CONTENTS

PREFACE

About this book

The main purposes of the School Physics in Engineering Project and its books are:
* to show ways in which physics that pupils study in their GCSE courses is used in practice;
* to provide real numerical examples and problems for class work and homework, derived from the engineering which has been described;
* to interest pupils in engineering.

These are central features of the aims of GCSE courses in physics.

This book describes some of the ways in which engineers make use of a knowledge of heat and temperature in their everyday work.

The contexts of internal combustion engines and construction sites have been chosen for heat and temperature because between them they provide examples which cover almost every part of this section of 13 years to 16 years syllabuses. Also, internal combustion engines and local construction activities are ready to hand for most pupils and most schools.

The book is intended as a complement to the physics textbook that is in class use in a school. It aims to show how physics that a class is being taught is used in practice. It does not set out to teach the physics although it provides revision summaries of key parts of syllabuses. The Narrative Section of the book uses heat engines and construction examples to link practice with physics principles. Calculations are few and simple. The Development Section extends the relationship between the physics and the engineering, and it gives numerical examples and problems. The problems are carefully graded. Numerical answers are provided.

The book can be used in different ways. The Narrative Section can be used to introduce the class teaching of a syllabus section of physics; or it can be used after the teaching for emphasis of key features. The examples and problems in the Development Section can be used for class work or for homework. They can complement the questions in the class textbook.

PHYSICS IN ACTION

Heat and Temperature

GORDON RAITT
Director, School Physics in Engineering Project

The right of the
University of Cambridge
to print and sell
all manner of books
was granted by
Henry VIII in 1534.
The University has printed
and published continuously
since 1584.

CAMBRIDGE UNIVERSITY PRESS

Cambridge

New York New Rochelle Melbourne Sydney

Published by the Press Syndicate of the University of Cambridge
The Pitt Building, Trumpington Street, Cambridge CB2 1RP
32 East 57th Street, New York, NY 10022, USA
10 Stamford Road, Oakleigh, Melbourne 3166, Australia

First published 1987

Printed in Great Britain by Scotprint Ltd, Musselburgh, Scotland

British Library cataloguing in publication data
Raitt, Gordon
Heat and temperature.——(Physics in action)
1. Heat
I. Title   II. Series
536   QC255

Library of Congress catalogue card number: 86-26876

ISBN 0 521 31087 3

GK

The cover shows a bimetal thermometer with dial readout (see page 30).

The School Physics in Engineering Project

The main purposes of the Project were given in the previous section: 'About this Book'.

The initial work was done in the Physics Department of a large comprehensive school from 1979 to 1983, with $7/10$ teaching and $3/10$ curriculum development programmes. Regular visits were made to construction sites, and visits to manufacturing companies. Modules were written, and were used with classes in three comprehensive schools. Evaluation returns from the schools have formed a basis for revising and extending the texts, and for developing them into book form. This last stage, which has included further industrial visits, was carried out during an attachment to the Department of Education of the University of Southampton, 1983–1985.

In order to ensure technical accuracy, each section of the texts together with its photographs and diagrams was sent to several assessors. These included a combination of site engineers, engineers in companies whose machinery has been described, polytechnic staff and university staff.

The work has been funded by the Industry Education Unit of the Departments of Trade and Industry, the Comino Foundation, The Cement and Concrete Association, Dow Mac Concrete Ltd, Paterson Candy International Ltd, The Precast Concrete Industry Training Association, and by a loan from West Sussex County Council. This funding made the Development possible, by providing release time during industrial working hours for the necessary visits, and by providing a final period of fulltime working to complete the Project. I am very grateful indeed for the support of these sponsors of the work.

Acknowledgments

In this book, much of the information on internal combustion engines has been obtained from Perkins Engines Ltd and I am grateful to the company and its staff. The construction work examples are from four sites. I am grateful to the owners of the sites, including West Sussex County Council, the Southern Water Authority, and the Department of the Environment, and to the contractors: French Keir Construction Limited, Norwest Holst Ltd, and Willett Ltd for arrangements to visit the sites regularly and follow the work.

Dr J.W. Warren of the Department of Physics, Brunel University, kindly read the draft text and his detailed comments have enabled me to clarify and improve a number of aspects. I am very grateful to him.

Table of units

Unit	Symbol
millimetre	mm
centimetre	cm
metre	m
kilometre	km
gram	g
kilogram	kg
tonne	t
second	s
minute	min
watt	W
kilowatt	kW
joule	J
hertz	Hz

Narrative section

Engineers and heat

Engineers spend a great deal of time thinking about heat and temperature. Most of the power for industry, for construction, and for our homes is produced by 'heat engines', such as diesel engines, petrol engines, and steam turbines. Most of them use a fuel such as diesel oil, petrol, or coal, which they burn with air to produce heat. Some of them use nuclear fuel. Even if our home or a factory is 'all electric', the electricity is produced by a steam turbine which drives the alternator that generates the electricity.

Electrical engineers have to think about heat and temperature. They may be designing an electric motor to drive a piece of machinery, so using electricity to do work. The electric current in the windings of the motor will produce heat, and if this is not removed from the motor fast enough the temperature will rise and the motor will become damaged. So the electrical engineers design the motor in a way that allows the heat to escape fast enough.

Whatever job an engineer is doing, it will involve machines or equipment that do work; and when work is done **some heat is always produced.** Moreover, **some of this heat is always lost.** Engineers do their designing so as to use heat in the most effective way that they can.

Power for machinery

Several years before engineers start work on a construction site they must plan the operation. One of the most important parts of the planning is to work out the cost. The construction of a bypass round a small town involved building just over 4 kilometres of new roadway and a bridge over a river. The river is 35 metres wide, and the bridge is about 100 metres from one end to the other. The total cost in the early 1980s was about £2 500 000. The main ways in which the money was used are shown in Table 1.

From Table 1 we can see that the second most costly item was providing vehicles and mechanical plant, at 22% of the total. These machines had to be provided with fuel. What percentage of the total cost was spent in fuel for the machines? And what percentage of the total cost was therefore spent in providing machines and keeping them going? All of this machinery is powered by heat engines, mainly diesel engines.

1

Table 1 This shows the main ways in which money was needed for building a 100 m long bridge and 4 km of new road.

Percentage of total cost, %	How the money was used
30	PAY for employees
22	Vehicles and mechanical plant: (lorries, dumpers, excavators, cranes, and medium and small machinery)
19	Road materials: (graded stone mixtures and bitumen / stone mixtures)
8	Reinforcing steel
8	Cement
3	Fuel for vehicles and mechanical plant
2	Timber
8	Miscellaneous
100	

Some heat engines

Figure 1 shows an excavator at work. It has been designed for digging holes and trenches for foundations, and for pipes or cables. The digging arm is operated hydraulically, by oil at high pressure acting on pistons. The power for operating the hydraulic digging systems, and the power for moving the 12 tonne

Figure 1 A hydraulic excavator is at work. The engine is at the lefthand end; it is a six-cylinder diesel, producing 73 kW of power.

excavator along on its tracks comes from a six-cylinder diesel engine. This engine is mounted on the lefthand end of the excavator and it can develop 73 kilowatts of power. This power is equivalent to eight 125 cc motor cycles at full power. (A 125 cc motor cycle develops about 12 brake horse power, and 1 hp = ¾ kilowatt, so a 125 cc motor cycle develops about 9 kilowatts of power).

Figure 2 shows a water pump being used to pump out an unfinished section of drains for a road under construction. The water travels along the righthand hosepipe and enters the bottom of the pump. The water leaves the top of the pump and goes along the lefthand hosepipe. On the left of the pump is the engine, which is a one-cylinder diesel that can give 4.5 kW of power to the pump. This is equivalent to half of the power of a 125 cc motor cycle at full throttle.

Figure 2   In the foreground is a water pump at work. The pump is on the right of the machine, and the engine to drive it is on the left. It is a one-cylinder diesel, providing 4.5 kW of power.

Internal combustion engines and energy

When a fuel is burned with air, energy is released. Table 2 shows the energy released when some common fuels are completely burned in air. The figures are for 1 kilogram of fuel, and the energy is measured in joules.

From Table 2 we see that 1 kg of the common liquid fuels gives out about 45 000 000 J of energy when it is completely burned. To do this it needs oxygen from the air, and the fuel burns to give carbon dioxide and steam. Using the liquid fuel heptane (which is closely related to octane) as an example, the chemical reaction is this:

$$C_7H_{16} \quad + \quad 11O_2 \quad \rightarrow \quad 7CO_2 \ + 8H_2O$$

| Heptane fuel | Oxygen | Carbon | Steam |
| 1 kg | | dioxide | |

and about 46 000 000 J of energy is given out.

3

Table 2   The energy which is produced by completely burning 1 kg of some fuels in air (1 kg of the liquid fuels occupies approximately 1¼ litres).

Fuel	Energy from burning 1 kg of fuel	
	joules, J	kilojoules, kJ
Coal	25 000 000	25 000
Anthracite	30 000 000	30 000
Diesel oil	45 000 000	45 000
Paraffin (kerosine)	46 000 000	46 000
Petrol	47 000 000	47 000

Figure 3   This is a paraffin stove using liquid fuel to produce heat.

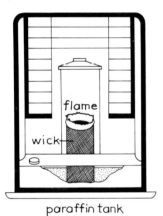

paraffin tank

If the liquid fuel is burned in the open atmosphere in a special burner, such as paraffin in a paraffin stove, then energy is produced which can be used to heat a room. In such an arrangement, however, no useful work is done.

A large paraffin heater in a youth club hut burns ½ kg of paraffin an hour. How many joules of energy does it give out per hour? You can use Table 2.

Figure 3 shows a paraffin stove burning fuel to heat a room; but no work is being done.

Liquid fuel could be burned another way. Figure 4 shows this happening. It could be mixed with air and fed into a chamber consisting of a cylinder and a piston. The fuel and oxygen mixture

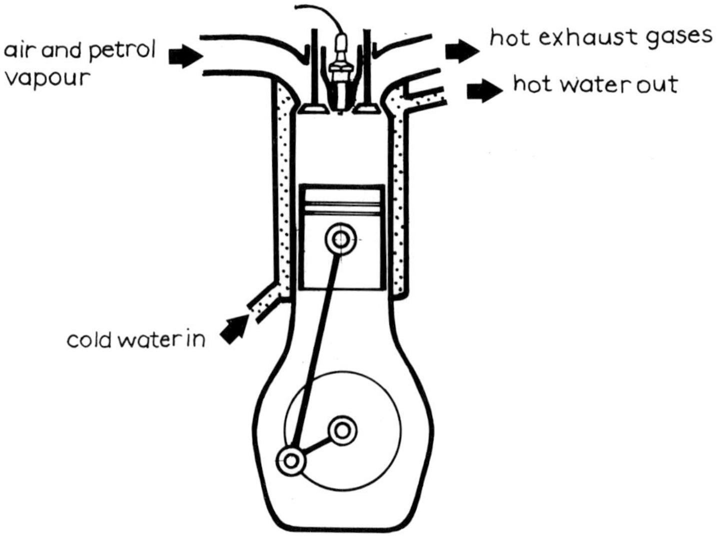

Figure 4   This is an internal combustion engine using liquid fuel to do useful work.

in the cylinder could then be ignited by a spark from a spark plug. The mixture would burn explosively; the heat that is given out would cause the temperature of the gases to rise. The pressure of the gases on the piston would increase, and the piston would be driven down.

The moving piston could be attached to a crankshaft and be made to do work. This is the principle of the petrol engine and the diesel engine.

At first sight it might seem that if a petrol engine uses up 1 kg of petrol then the engine will do 47 000 000 J of work (according to Table 2). But this is not so. It is a heat engine, and it works by producing gases at high temperatures. These gases have to be removed through the exhaust pipe, and the temperature of the gases as they enter the exhaust pipe is about 600 °C, depending on the engine. A great deal of energy is therefore lost through the exhaust as heat.

Also the cylinders are in contact with the high temperature gases, and the cylinders would become overheated and damaged if a cooling system were not provided. In motor cycle engines, air is used to cool the cylinder. Some cars and lorries have air-cooled engines, others have water-cooled engines. Much heat is carried away in the cooling air or the cooling water. In fact, so much energy is lost that out of the energy which the burning fuel and air can give only about 25% is available for doing work. Petrol engines are about 25% efficient, and diesel engines are about 35% efficient.

Engineers who design and manufacture heat engines do laboratory tests on the engines to find out where the energy of the fuel and air mixture goes. This is called doing an energy balance on the engine. Table 3 is a typical energy balance for a diesel engine.

Another way of looking at an energy balance is to think what volumes of fuel are used and lost. Figure 5 shows this: it represents a fuel tank of volume 100 litres. For every 100 litres of diesel fuel bought for the engine, only 35 litres do useful work.

Figure 5 This shows how 100 litres of fuel is used up in a diesel engine.

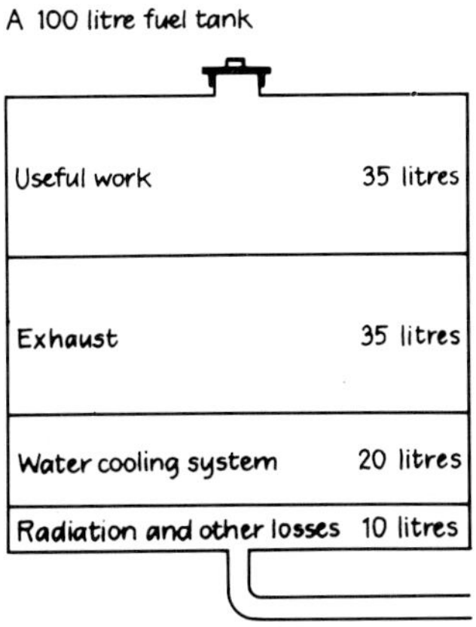

A 100 litre fuel tank

Useful work	35 litres
Exhaust	35 litres
Water cooling system	20 litres
Radiation and other losses	10 litres

Table 3 This is an energy balance for a diesel engine. It is the result of laboratory tests on the engine. (Because the total is 100, the figures in the righthand column are also percentages.)

Energy provided by the diesel fuel burning / million J	How the energy goes. Found by experiment / million J	
100	Useful work	35
	Heat in exhaust gases	35
	Heat in cooling water	20
	Heat radiation and other heat losses	10
		100

Thirty-five litres are used in producing the heat that goes out through the exhaust. The heat from 20 litres of fuel is carried away in the engine cooling water; and the heat from 10 litres is lost by radiation, and in other ways.

Most petrol engines are about 25% efficient. The exact efficiency depends upon the make of the engine. If the petrol engine is water-cooled, suggest some figures for the percentage of energy which does **useful work**, and the percentages which are lost through **the exhaust, the cooling water**, and **radiation and other ways**.

Energy changes and efficiency

A mobile lighting tower

Figure 6 shows a mobile lighting tower with four 1 500 watt floodlights. The heavy crane travels in sections on several lorries, and has to be assembled when it reaches a site. The mobile lighting tower had been placed in position to enable the crane crew to assemble the crane during the night, so that the crane would be ready for lifting bridge beams early next morning.

The floodlights are powered by electricity from a generator which is mounted on the same trailer as the telescopic lighting tower, and the generator is shown in Figures 7 and 8. On the left is a two-cylinder diesel engine which can generate 9 kilowatts of mechanical power output. Coupled to it, on the right, is an alternator. When the alternator is turned by the diesel engine, it produces alternating current and can deliver 7 kW of electrical power.

In each lamp, the electric current heats a tungsten filament which becomes white-hot and gives out light.

Figure 8 shows the steps in going from the energy of a fuel and air mixture to the energy of light radiation. At each step, the energies can be measured. Let us look at what happens to 100 joules of energy from the fuel and air mixture.

Figure 6 On the right of the photograph is a mobile telescopic lighting tower. It has four electric floodlights.

Figure 7 This is the electricity generator at the foot of the lighting tower in Figure 6. The 9 kW diesel engine can produce 7 kW of electric power.

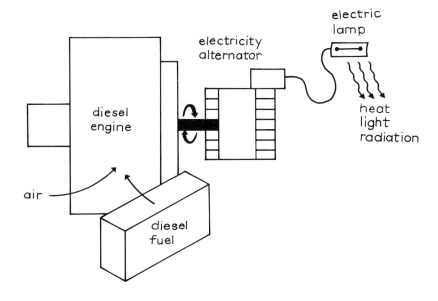

Figure 8 This diagram shows the main stages in using diesel fuel to produce light from electricity.

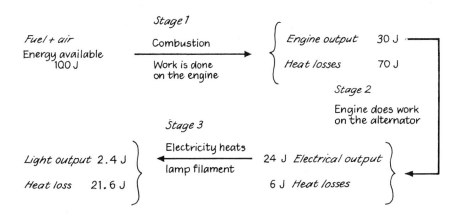

For every 100 J of energy that we start with, from the fuel and air, we get 2.4 J of light energy. The overall process is 2.4% efficient.

Let us have a look at each step.

$$\text{Efficiency} = \frac{\text{Useful energy got out}}{\text{Total energy put in}} = \frac{\text{Useful work got out}}{\text{Total energy put in}}$$

The **engine** uses 100 J of energy and does 30 J of useful work. What is the efficiency of the engine, as a percentage? From what you know about diesel engines does this seem about right?

30 J of work goes into the **alternator**, and the electrical output is 24 J. What is the efficiency of the alternator?

The electric current does 24 J of work on the **lamp filament**, and 2.4 J of light energy is given out. What is the efficiency of the change?

Have a look again at the three steps. Using some notepaper, add up the heat losses. What do they come to?

To this figure, add the light output. What does the total come to?

Does the total energy given out in all the steps equal the energy available at the start?

The least efficient step is the final one. The electric current does work on the filament, making it white-hot. Of the work done, only 10% gives light; the rest is lost as heat.

Efficiency and costs

When the overall efficiency is only about 2% we may well ask 'Why not make the system more efficient?' It is possible to make each step more efficient; but then each machine (engine, alternator and lamp) will cost more to design and to build, so each machine will cost more to buy. That is, the capital cost will be greater.

Much more efficient lamps than tungsten filament lamps are available, but they are more delicate. On a mobile lighting set that is going to be towed around, often over rough ground, the need is for sturdy lamps that will not become damaged.

A system of machines is usually designed and made to do a particular job. It is possible to design and make a cheap system which has one particular efficiency; and it is possible to design and build a more efficient but also more expensive system. After a certain point, the extra costs can be more than the savings which are made from the greater efficiency. Then the user would be losing money instead of saving it.

The manufacturing firms which provide machines and equipment for other people to use ask the users exactly what the machine or equipment must do. They also ask about the conditions under which the machine will have to work. On

Figure 9 This is an electricity generator. The 8-cylinder diesel engine can produce 270 kW of power, and it needs a large water cooling system; the 'radiator' is on the left. The alternator is on the right and can provide 250 kW of electric power. (Tripower Limited).

construction sites, it will be in the open, on rough ground. In the summer it will be exposed to sun and dust, and in the winter to rain. The engineers and technicians then design and build a machine that will do the job in the most effective way possible, taking into account machine efficiency, operating conditions, reliability, capital costs and running costs. This always needs imagination, ingenuity and skill, and a team of people working together.

Pile driving

On very many sites the soil is not strong enough to support the pressure of the structure which is to be built upon it. In these instances, piles are driven down to a firmer layer and the structure is then supported partly on the piles. In very soft ground it may be supported entirely on the piles.

Several different types of pile are manufactured. The ones in Figure 10 are in the form of pipes or tubes with concrete walls. The bottom of the pile is tapered to form a nose cone, so that the pile can be driven into the ground. In the foreground of Figure 10 several piles have already been driven down to firm rock, and their tops are visible. One pile is in the piledriver, and resting on its top is a steel 'helmet'. Above that is a 6t steel mass, suspended by a cable; this is a 'drop hammer'. It has gravitational potential energy because of its height above the helmet.

Figure 10 This shows a piledriver with a 6t drop hammer.

Figure 11 A cylinder of wood is used as a cushion, to soften the blow of the hammer.

9

If the 6t hammer were dropped directly onto the concrete pile, the pile would be damaged and would rapidly break up, so a cushion is used to soften the blow. The cushion consists of cylindrical blocks of wood placed in the helmet; one wood block can be seen in Figure 11. The cushion protects the pile, but of course it absorbs some of the energy of the dropping hammer.

Figure 12 shows a pile which has been driven down, and smoke is coming out of the helmet. The moving hammer has energy of motion, kinetic energy; and when the hammer hits the wood block some of the kinetic energy is converted into internal energy in the wood. As the hammering goes on, the wood gets hotter and hotter; and the temperature can become so high that the wood catches fire. It has done that here. Figure 13 shows the charred remains of a wooden cushion removed from the helmet.

As much as 20% to 30% of the kinetic energy of the hammer can be lost in generating heat in the cushion. Then as the blow is transmitted through the pile to the ground, the ground shakes or 'quakes'. A person standing 25 metres away can feel the ground quaking under his or her feet as the piledriving proceeds. As much as 30% of the hammer's energy can be lost in groundquake. The operator of the piledriver winches the 6t hammer up and then lets the cable run. As the hammer falls it has to pull the cable behind it, and this can result in a loss of 20% of energy in the friction of 'cable drag'. There are other energy losses as well; for instance, noise energy is produced.

Figure 12 The pile has been driven well down, and smoke is coming from the heated wooden cushion.

Figure 13 The charred remains of the wooden cushion

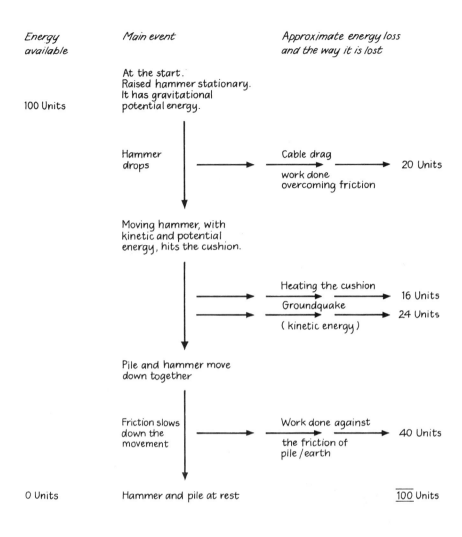

Figure 14 This shows the main events and the energy losses in the piledriving.

Energy available	Main event	Approximate energy loss and the way it is lost
100 Units	At the start. Raised hammer stationary. It has gravitational potential energy.	
	Hammer drops	Cable drag work done overcoming friction → 20 Units
	Moving hammer, with kinetic and potential energy, hits the cushion.	Heating the cushion → 16 Units Groundquake (kinetic energy) → 24 Units
	Pile and hammer move down together	
	Friction slows down the movement	Work done against the friction of pile/earth → 40 Units
0 Units	Hammer and pile at rest	100 Units

The stages and the main energy losses are shown in Figure 14.

Of the 100 Units of energy to start with, how much energy was actually available to drive down the pile? How efficient is this system as a user of energy?

What is the total of work done and energy lost (righthand column of Figure 14)? What was the energy available at the start?

If the 6 t hammer dropped 5 m, how much energy was used in each of the four main ways? Give the answer in joules.

Heat evolution: Concrete setting

The two most important materials in large-scale construction are concrete and steel. Engineers need to know the properties of these materials, so that they can make the best use of the materials.

Many different types of concrete and steel have been tested in laboratories and in field trials, and the results have been recorded for engineers to use.

One of the properties of freshly made concrete that engineers have to take into account is that it gives out heat as it sets.

A typical concrete consists of the materials shown in Table 4.

Table 4 Composition of a typical concrete.

Materials	Mass/kg
Dry gravel (maximum 2 cm across)	400
Dry sand	200
Cement powder	100 (2 standard bags)
Water	50 (50 litres)
Total	750

Figure 15 This shows the proportions by volume of the materials used in making concrete.

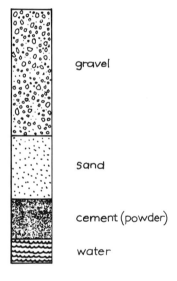

gravel

sand

cement (powder)

water

Figure 15 shows the proportions of the materials by volume.

These amounts of materials give ¾ tonne of concrete (750 kilogram), which would occupy a volume about 1 metre × 1 metre × ⅓ metre. The cement powder reacts chemically with the water and with the sand and gravel to form strong chemical bonds. These bonds bind the materials together, and as the bonds are formed, heat is given out. 100 kg of cement powder (2 standard bags) give out about 25 000 000 joules of heat when mixed as concrete and allowed to set. This heat raises the temperature of the concrete. Freshly made concrete can be poured into a well-insulated box, and thermometers can be used to measure its temperature. Figure 16 shows how the temperature rises during the first three days.

When does the temperature rise most rapidly: during the first day, the second day, or the third day? After three days, what was the rise in temperature, approximately? The amount of heat given out by 100 kg of cement powder in concrete varies depending on the type of cement, and so the temperature rise also varies. Experiments show that the rise can vary from about 20 K to about 40 K with different types of cement.

But is this information of any use? It is very important to engineers if they are pouring large volumes of fresh concrete to make a large structure. Figure 17 shows this being done.

About 1200 t of concrete is being poured, from the elevated hose and from the large bucket or skip, to form part of a bridge. The concrete is being poured into a space which is, in rounded-off figures, 30 m long × 10 m wide × 2 m deep. This huge mass of setting concrete generates heat and its temperature rises. Heat is lost rapidly from the outside of the mass, and slowly from the inside. After a while the inside of the concrete will be at a higher temperature than the outside, and this will set up strains which could cause the concrete to crack. Cracks could seriously weaken the structure.

Figure 16 The graph shows the temperature rise of insulated fresh concrete.

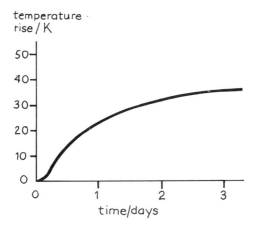

The situation cannot be left like this. What is one to do? In cold weather it may be necessary to insulate the outside of the concrete and thus slow down the rate at which heat is lost. In the work shown in Figure 17, the engineers left small spaces in the concrete at selected places. Thermometers were placed in these pockets, and the temperatures were recorded and watched carefully for several days.

Figure 17 A large mass of concrete is being poured into a wide, deep box, or formwork. It is to form part of a bridge. The temperature of the setting concrete will rise.

13

Some temperature measurements

Figure 18 shows a maximum and minimum thermometer mounted on the outside of a site office. The speed at which concrete sets depends on the temperature of the concrete and on the temperature of the surroundings, and engineers take readings and keep records of both.

Figure 18 A maximum and minimum thermometer is fixed on the outside of a site office. The air temperature is often needed.

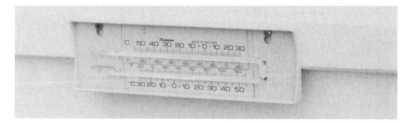

Cold concrete takes longer to set and to gain strength than does warm concrete, because the chemical reactions are slower at lower temperatures. If the weather is very cold, and the gravel, sand and cement powder are cold it may be necessary to heat the water that is used for making the concrete. The temperature of the atmosphere must therefore be known.

The temperature of the atmosphere can also be too high for good setting. On a hot summer day, water will evaporate rapidly from the surface of the concrete; and the upper layer can soon have too little water, become weak and develop cracks. So, in hot dry weather, exposed surfaces of fresh concrete are often covered with a layer of wet sacking. Not only does the wet sacking keep the concrete damp, but also evaporation of water from the sacking causes a cooling and keeps the concrete cool. From time to time the sacking needs to be sprayed with water to replace the water that has evaporated.

Figure 19 A probe thermometer is being used to measure the temperature of setting concrete.

The ideal temperature for concrete to be poured is within a few degrees of 20°C. In Figure 19 a probe thermometer is being used to take the temperature of freshly poured concrete.

For this type of use, a sturdy thermometer is needed. The one shown has a stem which is a hollow steel tube and which is ¾m long. Inside the tube is a bimetal spiral, which moves when the temperature changes. (How this works is described on pages 30 to 31.)

Most survey instruments and equipment are manufactured to give correct readings at 20°C. If the temperature is much lower or much higher than 20°C, then the temperature should be read and corrections should be made to the survey readings.

(How this works is described on pages 30 to 31.)

Figure 20 A 5m aluminium staff is being used to measure a level. The staff is the correct length at 20°C but not at other temperatures.

In Figure 20 the engineer and assistant are finding the level of the foot of the trench. That is, they are finding how much lower or higher it is than a fixed reference mark on the site. They are using a staff, which is a rule, marked in metres and centimetres. This staff is made of aluminium and it is 5.000 m long at 20°C. On a very hot day, with the temperature at 40°C, the staff is 5.002 m long; it has expanded by 2 mm. On a very cold day, with the temperature at −10°C, the staff is only 4.997 m long; it has contracted by 3 mm.

For most levelling work on a site, an accuracy of 1 or 2 mm is not necessary; but for particularly accurate work the temperature would be read and the expansion or contraction of the staff allowed for.

15

In Figure 21 there are two pieces of equipment on the tripod stand. The upper one, rectangular in shape, is an electronic distance meter; and the one under it is a theodolite. The electronic distance meter is for measuring distances. It sends out a beam of infra-red rays. If this beam is reflected back to the meter, then the meter can work out the time of passage and hence the distance to the reflector.

The speed at which the electromagnetic radiation travels through the air depends upon the density of the air, and this depends upon the temperature of the air and the pressure of the atmosphere. If the distance being measured is more than 100 m, then the air temperature and the atmospheric pressure should be measured, and a correction should be made.

The meter in the photograph contains its own computer. The atmospheric temperature and pressure are entered, and the computer will make the correction. Also, if the operator enters 7; AVE; the meter will make seven distance readings, work out the average, make the atmospheric corrections, and then display the corrected average on the screen.

Expansion and contraction

Almost all materials expand when their temperatures are raised, and they contract when their temperatures are lowered. A rod of steel 1 metre long raised in temperature from 10 °C to 11 °C, that is, through a temperature difference of 1 K, expands by 0.00001 metres, or $\frac{1}{100}$ millimetre. This may not seem to be very much, but if the material is 20 m or 30 m long, and if the temperature changes by 10 K or 20 K or more, then the expansion or contraction can be substantial.

Pipes for superheated water

Figure 22 shows hot water supply pipes being laid for a district heating system. The pipes are laid on small-size gravel, and they are surrounded by gravel. The pipes can move in this when they expand and contract; but they have to be fixed at certain places along their length. The pipes in Figure 22 are fixed in a concrete block at the top righthand corner of the photograph, where they turn a bend. They are also fixed in a concrete block just out of sight beyond the bottom lefthand corner of the photograph. The distance between the fixed points is 30 m.

The system supplies hot water at a pressure well above atmospheric pressure. It is at a total pressure of about 3 atmospheres, in the boiler and in the pipes. At this pressure, water does not boil at 100 °C but at about 130 °C, so the water can be pumped through the feed pipe at, say, 110 °C without it boiling; and this is the temperature used for this hot feed water.

Let us suppose that on the day when the pipes were laid the temperature of the atmosphere was 10 °C. Later, when the pipes are operating, the feed pipe will be at 110 °C. This temperature is

Figure 22 These are hot water supply pipes. Each has an expansion and contraction loop.

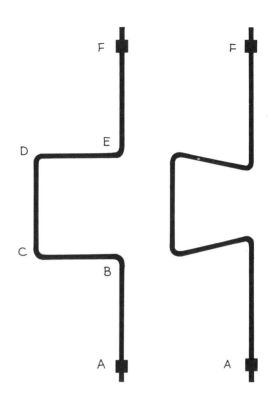

Figure 23 When the length of a pipe changes, bending takes place at the loop.

100 K higher than when the pipe was laid. A straight pipe 30 m long, rising in temperature through 100 K, would expand by over 30 mm. This would generate very great forces which would either break down the concrete supports at each end of the 30 m length, or break the welds at pipe joints, or buckle the pipe. Or it might do all three of these.

Some way must be found which will allow expansion and contraction to take place without doing any damage. One way is to form a loop in the pipe layout; a large loop can be seen in the photograph in Figure 22.

The way it works is shown in Figure 23. The pipe is fixed at A and at F. As the temperature rises, the length AB increases and the length FE increases. B and E move closer together; there is space for this to happen. At the same time, the loop becomes slightly bent; steel is flexible and allows this to happen. When the pipe cools down, movements take place in reverse.

If you live in an area where there are factories or works with outside pipes which carry hot liquids, look for expansion and contraction loops. The loops may be horizontal, like the ones in Figure 22; but very often they are vertical, and then they may be easy to see. If you find some of these pipes, do they seem to be bare or to be covered with insulation? Why?

17

Bridge beams

Bridge beams increase in length when their temperature rises, and decrease in length when their temperature falls. Engineers must take this into account when designing and constructing bridges. The beams must be allowed to move, so there must be a low friction support for each beam, and there must be space for the movement to occur, called an expansion gap. One method is to fix one end of the beam on its support, and to allow the other end to slide on a low friction bearing.

Figure 24 This is the concrete support for bridge beams. The technician is fixing bearing pads. Each has a low friction upper surface.

Figure 25 Here a bridge beam is being moved into position. It is 27 m long. (Manufactured by Dow Mac Concrete, Limited.)

Figure 24 shows an abutment for a small bridge. The abutment is the reinforced concrete structure at one end of the bridge which will support the beams. The technician is fixing the lower parts of the bearings. Each part is a rectangular pad with an upper surface of very smooth Teflon plastic (PTFE, polytetrafluorethylene). In the far corner of the abutment, beyond the technician's hands, two of the rectangular pads have already been fixed.

The end of the beam will have two rectangular steel plates on its underside, and each steel plate will have a highly polished smooth surface. When the beam is lowered into place, each smooth steel surface will rest on a smooth PTFE surface, forming a support with very little friction between the faces.

Figure 25 shows a beam being lowered into position. The two steel plates underneath one end are already fixed to it. The beam is 27 m long, and if its temperature changes from −10 °C in a winter cold spell to 25 °C during a summer heatwave, the length of the beam will increase by just over 10 mm.

Between the end wall of the concrete abutment and the end of the beam there must be a wide enough expansion gap to allow this to happen.

On the right of Figure 26 is the end of a beam; the dark black line is the expansion gap; and the engineer has his hands on the end wall of the bridge, the abutment. He is looking at the expansion gap, which is about 20 mm wide.

Figure 26 The engineer has his hands on the end wall of the bridge, the abutment. On the extreme right is a bridge beam. Between them is the expansion gap (the dark line).

Buildings with long walls

The outside wall of a building rises in temperature when the sun shines on it and falls in temperature during the night. In doing so, the wall expands and contracts. The main effect of the changes in length is at each end of the wall, where it joins another wall at right angles to it. The alternate pushing and pulling can cause cracks to develop at the junction of the walls. Building regulations which came into operation in the early 1980s in the United Kingdom require long walls in buildings to have an expansion gap every 12 m.

Figure 27 shows such an expansion gap. At the 12 m mark the bricks are no longer bonded, or made to overlap; instead, a gap is formed. Into this gap is placed fibre board, which fills the gap but which is soft and will squash when the walls expand and cause the gap to narrow. To keep the wall watertight, mastic is placed outside the fibre board.

Have a look at a building which has been constructed since 1980, or one that is being built at present. Look for the expansion gaps. How many expansion gaps are there along a wall? Are they at about every 12 m?

Figure 27 The photograph shows an expansion gap in the wall of a building.

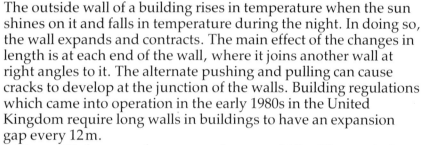

Reducing losses of heat: Insulation

Heat travels from a warm place to a colder place. In winter, the inside of a warmed house is at a higher temperature than the outside. Heat travels from the place at the higher temperature, the inside of the house, to the place at the lower temperature, the outside of the house, and there it becomes lost in the atmosphere.

To keep up the temperature inside the house, this lost energy has to be replaced, by burning oil fuel or gas, or by using electric heating, so the heat losses cost money. An average three- or four-bedroom house which is poorly insulated can lose heat worth several hundreds of pounds each year. By improving the

19

insulation, the amount of heat lost can be reduced and so the fuel costs can be reduced.

Table 5 gives approximate figures for heat losses for two houses of identical design. One is not insulated and the other is well-insulated, with insulation in the cavity walls and in the loft, with some double glazing and with draught excluders. If £100 is needed to keep the uninsulated house at a certain temperature for a certain number of weeks, only £55 is required to keep the insulated house at the same temperature for the same number of weeks.

Table 5 shows where the money goes; in an uninsulated house most of it goes out through the walls and the roof.

Figure 28 shows the cavity wall of a building, with a block of insulation. Other blocks of insulation will be placed, the outer

Table 5 Where the money goes in heat losses from two houses of the same size. Each house is kept at the same inside temperature.

Route of heat loss	Uninsulated house	Well-insulated house
Walls	£35	£10
Roof	£25	£10
Draughts	£15	£10
Ground	£15	£15
Windows	£10	Less than £10
Total	£100	£55

Figure 28 The cavity wall of a building is being made. The cavity has a block of insulation material in it. Other blocks of insulation will be placed, and will fill the cavity.

wall will be built up, and there will be insulation filling the cavity. This particular insulation is 'Rockwool'. It is a mineral wool, and between the fibres there are many small pockets of trapped air. These trapped air pockets are a very bad conductor of heat and so they make very good insulation.

Physicists and engineers have done laboratory experiments and site trials with different building materials and with different kinds of insulation to find the rates at which heat is conducted through them. The results have been recorded in tables so that architects and engineers can calculate heat losses for buildings. They can then make decisions about designs, and about how powerful a heating system to install.

Figure 29 shows the results of some of these experiments. If a room has a window made of typical glass, and if the temperature of the air in the room is 10°C and the temperature of the air outside is 0°C, then the temperature difference is 10 K. The experiments show that through 1 metre^2 of the window, heat escapes at the rate of 50 joules per second; that is, 50 watts.

The experiments also show that if the difference in temperature between the inside and the outside is doubled, then the rate of heat flow is doubled. If the air temperature in the room is raised to 20°C and if the temperature outside remains at 0°C, the

20

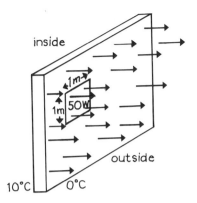

Figure 29 This shows a sheet of glass in a window. Heat is escaping. Fifty watts of power is escaping from each m² of surface; that is, 50 J/s.

temperature difference is now 20 K. The heat loss doubles and rises from 50 J/s to 100 J/s through every m² of window. This is 100 W/m².

An inside temperature of 30 °C and and an outside temperature of 10 °C again gives a temperature difference of 20 K, and the rate of loss of heat is the same as in the previous example, 100 W/m².

Figure 30 shows typical values for the rates at which heat is lost through four structures. The temperature difference between the inside air and the outside air is 10 K, and the figures for the power loss are for each m² of outer surface. In practice, the values vary depending upon the type of materials: how the wood door is made, the type of bricks in the walls, and the type of insulation used in the cavity of the wall.

How much heat is actually lost from a building per second, under typical conditions? We can work this out for a simple building such as a site office.

Figure 30 This shows power losses through four structures, per m² of outer surface, for a 10 K temperature difference between one side and the other.

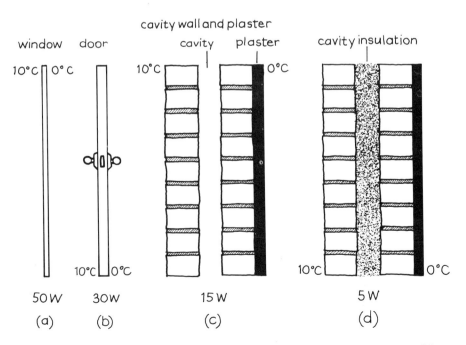

Figure 31 This shows a portable site office.

Figure 31 shows a portable building which is being used as an office while construction proceeds. Companies which manufacture portable buildings make them as units; inside, they can be arranged for many different uses. Internal partitions can be fixed to make large or small rooms. Electricity can be installed for lighting and heating, and plumbing can be installed.

The men and women who are at work on the site must have suitable accommodation, and the portable units will be arranged to provide a variety of warm, comfortable rooms. There will be a kitchen and canteen. There will be showers and toilets. A conference room will be needed for meetings; and there will be several offices, and perhaps a small drawing office. There will be a reception and secretarial room, with a telephone switchboard and typewriter.

The building in Figure 31 measures 2 m high × 3 m wide × 9 m long. The walls are of cavity construction, like the walls of a house, and are made with thick plywood. The cavity is 60 mm wide and is filled with fibre glass matting insulation. The roof is similarly constructed. The floor is thick plywood with a vinyl covering. Information about the transfer of heat through the walls, roof, and floor is provided by the manufacturer. Figure 32 shows the rate at which heat is lost from the building. The average is about 6 W/m², if there is a temperature difference of 10 K between the air inside and the air outside. What is the average power loss for the insulated cavity wall of a house, per m² of wall? Figure 30 gives a value. For a light, portable building would you say that the site office compares well with the house?

Let us calculate the rate of loss of heat from the office if the air is at a temperature of 10 °C inside and at 0 °C outside. Then 6 W are lost through every m² of surface.

Area of near end	= 2 m × 3 m	=	6 m²
Area of far end	= 2 m × 3 m	=	6 m²
Area of roof	= 3 m × 9 m	=	27 m²
Area of floor	= 3 m × 9 m	=	27 m²
Area of 2 sides	= 2 m × 9 m × 2 =		36 m²
Total area		=	102 m²

22

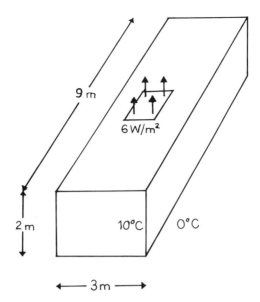

Figure 32 Calculating the rate at which heat is lost from the site office in Figure 31.

Therefore, total power loss $= 6\,\text{W/m}^2 \times 102\,\text{m}^2 = 612\,\text{W}$. So 612 W of power is being lost. That is, 612 J of heat are escaping each second. In order to keep the temperature of the office at 10°C, heat would have to be replaced at this rate, so a small heater of 612 W power would be needed.

In fact, 10°C is a rather low temperature for a room; 20°C is more comfortable. If the outside temperature remains at 0°C, the temperature difference is now 20 K instead of 10 K, and heat will be escaping at twice the rate (12 W per m² of surface). Twice as much power will therefore be needed to replace the lost heat and a heater of power 2 × 612 W will be needed. This is 1224 W, or 1.224 kW, so a 2 kW convector heater would be adequate.

This calculation has looked at the building as a box without windows, and without a door. The building actually has windows with a total area of 7 m². Have a look at the power loss values for window glass given in Figure 30. If the windows are closed, will their existence in the office mean that more power is lost, or less, than in our calculation? Will the heater have to be turned up or down?

If the temperature is 10°C inside the office and 0°C outside, what is the rate of heat loss through the 7 m² of windows?

Since breathing uses up air, fresh air has to be allowed into a room. The official United Kingdom guideline is that an office should have one air change per hour. A school classroom should have two changes per hour. If the air outside is colder than the air inside, then this fresh air will have to be heated.

Measure a window in your house or flat. Estimate or measure the temperature inside, and that outside. Calculate the rate of heat loss through the window. If you have double glazing, use 25 W instead of the 50 W in Figure 29 and Figure 30.

Choose a room in your house or flat. Measure the wall area of the outside wall or walls, and the window area.

(a) Calculate the rate of heat loss when the outside temperature is 0°C and the inside temperature is 20°C.

(b) At what rate will heat have to be supplied to the room to keep it at 20°C?

(c) How many kW is this?

(d) If the room is kept at 20°C for a day and a night, that is, 24 hours, how many kW hours of energy is needed?

(e) Ask to look at a recent electricity bill, and find from it the cost of 1 kW hour of work done electrically.

(f) How much does it cost to keep the room at 20°C for 24 hours?

Increasing losses of heat: Cooling systems

An engine cooling system

Internal combustion engines, that is, petrol engines and diesel engines, burn a fuel in their cylinders. The flame of the burning petrol or diesel fuel is very hot, and the temperature of the gases in the cylinders can be about 2000°C. The heat released heats up the neighbouring parts of the engine, and this causes problems.

The pistons must be able to move freely in their cylinders, and they are therefore lubricated by oil. Lubricating oils, however, begin to break down chemically if their temperature rises above about 200°C. Also, the cylinders and cylinder heads are made of metals or alloys whose strength begins to decrease above about 200°C.

Therefore the temperature of the cylinders and cylinder heads has to be kept below 200°C, and a cooling system is needed. This cooling system must carry away heat, in order to keep the temperature down. Some engines are air-cooled and some are water-cooled.

Figure 33 This shows the principle of a water cooling system in a four-cylinder engine. Temperature differences cause the water to circulate. (An air fan and a water pump have been left out of the diagram for simplicity.)

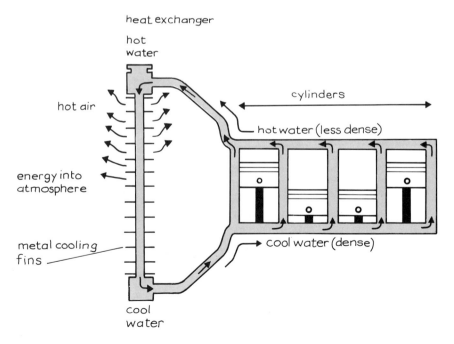

heat exchanger

hot water

hot air

cylinders

hot water (less dense)

energy into atmosphere

metal cooling fins

cool water (dense)

cool water

Table 3 on page 5 shows the main ways in which the energy from the explosions of the air and diesel fuel in a diesel engine is used and is lost. About 35% of the energy which can be got from the fuel and air mixture can do useful work, and the rest is lost: about 35% in exhaust gases, about 20% in the cooling water, and about 10% through radiation and other causes.

Figure 33 shows the principle of a water cooling system. The cylinders are surrounded by water-jackets with spaces in them, so that water can circulate. When the engine is running, the hot cylinders raise the temperature of the water around them. This water expands. In doing so it becomes less dense, and rises up the jacket, into the top channel, and up a pipe to the top of the radiator.

The radiator is a group of vertical metal tubes with metal fins. The hot water in the upper part of the radiator heats the metal tubes and the metal fins. These fins then heat the air around them, and energy is transferred into the atmosphere. In these ways, energy is lost from the water and the water cools.

As the water cools it becomes denser and sinks; and so a convection current is set up.

The vertical tubes and their fins are a **heat exchanger**. They enable the hot water to exchange heat with the cooler air. Most of this exchange occurs by the processes of **conduction** and **convection**. Very little is done by **radiation**, so 'radiator' is not a good name for this part of a vehicle.

In most water-cooled engines there is a fan to draw or blow air through the radiator cooling fins; and there is a water pump to improve the water circulation. Have a look at Figure 9.

Examine a motor cycle engine and look at the cooling fins. Ask the owner of a car if you may look at the cooling system. For safety, ensure that the engine is **not** running (so that the fan and drive belts are stationary). Also, make sure that the engine is **cool**. The radiator cap should **not** be taken off if the engine is hot; boiling water could burst out. Have a look at the radiator. Find the entry pipe for the hot water. Find the exit pipe for the cooler water. Look at the fins.

Look at the fan. How is the fan driven round?

Ask the owner where the water pump is (or consult the vehicle handbook). How is the water pump driven?

Conduction, convection, and radiation

Heat is a process in which energy is transferred from a body at one temperature to another body **at a lower temperature**; and the transfer happens because of the temperature difference.

In the heat exchanger, heat is transferred through the metal tube walls and along the metal fins by **conduction**.

Inside the tubes of the heat exchanger, heat is carried by **convection** currents. At the top of the exchanger, the hot water loses energy along the fins and the water becomes cooler. As it becomes cooler, the water becomes more dense; and it sinks down the vertical pipes towards the bottom of the exchanger. It continues to lose heat on the way, and to become cooler and denser.

When the cool water reaches the cylinders it becomes heated. It expands, becomes less dense and rises. Because of the density changes in the water as it becomes heated and then cooled, a continuous circulation of water is set up. It is a water **convection current.**

Air convection takes most of the heat away from the heat exchanger into the atmosphere. The hot metal fins warm up the air, and the air expands, becomes less dense, and moves upwards and away from the fins.

If a car is moving forwards, air is forced between the fins; and a flow of cool air goes through the heat exchanger. This is **forced convection.** In addition, an engine has a fan to draw air through the heat exchanger; this is another form of forced convection. Figure 48 on page 46 shows an engine with a fan for the heat exchanger. It also has a water pump to provide forced convection in the water system.

A little energy is lost from the fins through electromagnetic waves, mainly infra-red waves. This is **radiation**.

Heat exchanger fins

The purpose of the metal fins on the exchanger is to increase the surface area of metal from which heat can be passed to the atmosphere. A single pipe has a certain surface area, but the same pipe with fins attached to it has a very much larger surface area. This makes it a much more efficient cooling device.

Compressed air

Compressed air is a very convenient way of transferring energy. Work has to be done in order to compress air. The compressed air can be led through a hose to an engine, for instance a turbine engine or a piston engine, and made to do work.

Compressed air is used to provide the power for a very wide range of equipment and tools, from two-tonne hammers for piledriving to small hand-held drills, cutters and grinders.

Figure 34 shows an air compressor being used to work a small air-driven hammer. This hammer is driving steel posts into the ground at the side of a road under construction.

Figure 35 shows concrete being poured to form reinforced concrete for a bridge. The box, or formwork, into which it is being poured is about 1½ metres deep here, and there are hundreds of steel rods carefully placed in the formwork. The fluid concrete must fill all the cavities, and come into close contact with all of the reinforcing steel. Some of the concrete, however, has become held up on the steel rods, and is not going down into the spaces. It could be pushed and shaken with a spade, but this would be a slow and ineffective method. The man on the right of the

Figure 34 An air compressor is providing power for a compressed air hammer.

Figure 35 Fluid concrete is being piped to the reinforcing steel rods of a bridge. The man on the right is holding a hose supplying compressed air to a concrete vibrator.

photograph is holding a hose; it carries compressed air to a mechanical vibrator, which looks like a slightly thicker part of the hose and is just entering the concrete. The vibrator shakes the pasty concrete at a rate of about 200 vibrations per second, a frequency of 200 hertz. This changes the pasty concrete into a much more runny material, which now flows down between the rods.

When the fluid concrete has gone down below the surface, the operator lowers the vibrator into the meshwork of steel rods and continues to keep the concrete on the move. He does this until the concrete has flowed into all of the corners of the formwork and around the steel rods. The strength of the reinforced concrete will depend a great deal on how carefully the fluid is placed around the steel, and this stage in the work is very important. One of the largest uses of compressed air on construction sites is in driving concrete vibrators.

Bicycle pumps become warm

When a bicycle pump is being used to pump up a tyre, the barrel of the pump becomes warm; and this can be felt by the palm of the hand. The cyclist has to do work on the pump in order to force the piston down and compress the air in the pump barrel. This

Figure 36 The diagrams show uncompressed air, and rapidly compressed air.
(a) A cycle pump with air at atmospheric temperature and pressure.
(b) The piston forced down to compress the air into ⅓ of its former volume.

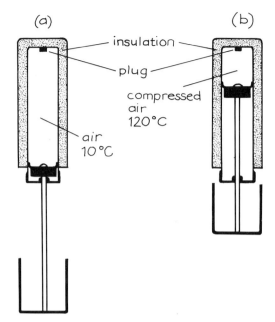

raises the temperature of the air, and heat becomes lost to the outside.

Figure 36 shows a bicycle pump. An airtight plug has been put in the delivery end, and the barrel has been surrounded by good insulation. At the start, in Figure 36(a), the barrel is full of air at a temperature of 10°C. The handle is quickly forced down to compress the air into only ⅓ of its previous volume, as in Figure 36(b), and the temperature of the air rises.

If no heat were absorbed by the barrel and by the end of the pump, and if no heat escaped, then the temperature of the air would rise to about 120°C, that is, above the boiling temperature of water.

Air compressors become hot

Figure 37 shows an air compressor like the one in Figure 34. In the centre, above the wheel, is the engine which provides the power for compressing the air; it is a four-cylinder diesel engine providing 43 kilowatts of power. On the left is the air compressor, marked HYDROVANE. It delivers air at a pressure of 7 atmospheres.

On being compressed, the air would reach a high temperature if it were not cooled in some way. The cooling arrangement is to have oil circulating in the compression chamber and around it. The oil cools the hot air, and keeps its temperature down to about 95°C. The hot air raises the temperature of the oil to about 95°C, so the oil has to be cooled before it can be used again. This is done by passing the hot oil through a heat exchanger.

For convenience, compactness and economy, the cooling fluid for the heat exchanger is the cool water from the water cooling system of the diesel engine that drives the compressor. When the compressor is working at full power, heat is being removed from

Figure 37 This is an air compressor. It provides compressed air at 7 atmospheres pressure. The compressor unit is on the left, and the diesel engine which drives it is in the centre.

the hot compressed air and is passed through the heat exchanger at the rate of 17 kW, or 17 000 joules per second.

The whole machine is an example of several companies working together. The compressor is designed and made by Hydrovane Compressor Company Ltd; the diesel engine is designed and made by Perkins Engines Ltd; and the oil/water heat exchanger is designed and made by Serck Heat Transfer Ltd. Fitting them together in a neat compact way to produce the final machine is done by Hydrovane Ltd.

Invent and sketch a simple system which has **a compressor** (perhaps like a bicycle pump), in which the compressor is **kept cool by oil**, which is taken away and **cooled by water**, which is **cooled by the atmosphere**. How many heat exchangers will your design need?

Compression ignition: diesel engines

In air compressors, the high temperature produced by compressing the air is a nuisance. In a diesel engine, however, it is the way in which the fuel and air mixture in the cylinder is made to ignite. A diesel engine does not have a spark plug; so there is no spark to cause the fuel and air to explode in the cylinder. Instead, the high temperature produced by compressing the air is used.

Figure 2, on page 3, shows a water pump driven by a single cylinder diesel engine. The air in the cylinder is compressed to 16 atmospheres pressure, and its temperature rises to about 600 °C. Diesel fuel is then injected, and the air/fuel mixture at the high temperature of 600 °C ignites and explodes.

Diesel engine fuel ignites by 'compression ignition'. Petrol engines need a spark plug and they work by 'spark ignition'.

You can read more about engines in other parts of this book. Pages 3 to 6, 'Internal Combustion Engines and Energy' describe where the energy for the engine comes from and where it goes. Pages 53 to 56, 'The Gas Laws', show how engineers can understand engines better, and how designs can be better if engineers know how gases behave.

A bimetal thermometer

Figure 38 This is a bimetal thermometer with a dial readout. The bimetal is inside the hollow steel stem, below the surface.

Figure 39 This shows a bimetal strip. One strip is made of an alloy 'Invar', S, and the other strip is made of iron, L. (a) At normal temperature.

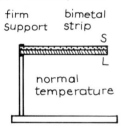

(b) Above normal temperature.

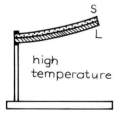

(c) Below normal temperature.

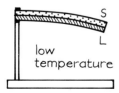

There are very many instances in industry where a mercury in glass thermometer is not suitable for measuring temperature. Mercury in glass thermometers are easily broken. The mercury is poisonous, and mercury thermometers are not allowed in the food processing industries, nor for many medical temperature measurements.

Where a strong, sturdy thermometer is needed, or if the thermometer has to be made of non-toxic materials, a bimetal thermometer may be a good choice.

Figure 38 shows a bimetal thermometer with a dial face. The bimetal is inside the lower end of the stem, deep in the material being tested. Figure 39 shows a bimetal strip, and the way in which it behaves when it is heated and cooled.

If a strip of the alloy 'Invar' is 10 metres long, and if its temperature is raised through $1\,K$ (say from $10\,°C$ to $11\,°C$) then the strip expands by 0.1 millimetres. If a strip of iron is $10\,m$ long and its temperature is raised through $1\,K$ the strip expands by $1.2\,mm$. That is, the expansion of the iron strip is 12 times the expansion of the Invar strip.

A **bimetal strip** is made by bonding strips of two different metals firmly together along their lengths. Figure 39 shows a strip of Invar, S, bonded to a strip of iron, L. In Figure 39 (a) the strips are at the normal or design temperature, and the two strips have the **same length**; the bimetal combination is **straight**.

If the temperature is raised, the iron strip, L, with the larger expansion property expands more than the Invar strip, S, with the smaller expansion property. The result is that the bimetal strip starts bending into a curve, as in Figure 39(b). The longer strip will be on the outside of the curve, where it covers the longer distance, as on a curved running track.

If the temperature is lowered below normal, then the iron strip contracts more than the Invar strip, so the bimetal strip curves downwards, with the shorter strip of iron on the inside of the curve. Equal changes of temperature produce equal changes in curvature, so this device can be used to make a thermometer.

Have a look at Figure 38 again. The hollow steel stem of the thermometer goes into the material about as far as it sticks out; and the bimetal strip is inside the bottom of the stem. Draw a sketch of what you think the thermometer might look like inside, from bottom to top; draw a longitudinal section.

This raises the question 'How can the movement of a bimetal strip at the bottom of the stem be conveyed to a pointer at the top of the stem?' Having the bimetal in the form of a straight strip causes difficulties.

One answer is to make the strip in the form of a flat spiral, like a clockwork clock spring. This is shown in Figure 40. At the inner end is a small metal hole; a spindle can be put into it. When the temperature changes, the spiral either coils up or uncoils. The spindle turns, and it could have a needle on its top end, moving over a dial.

When the temperature rises, does the spiral coil up or uncoil? Does the spindle rotate clockwise or anticlockwise?

Figure 40 This shows a bimetal strip made in the form of a flat spiral like a clockwork clock spring. S, Invar; L, iron.

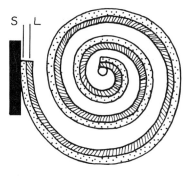

When the temperature falls, does the spiral coil up or uncoil? Does the spindle rotate clockwise or anticlockwise?

Another way of winding the bimetal is into a helix. Figure 41 shows some parts for making bimetal thermometers. Find in the photograph: a straight strip of bimetal; a flat coil of bimetal, with a spindle; a helix of bimetal; a helix with a base and a spindle; an indicator needle; a circular scale marked in °C.

Have a look again at the thermometer in Figure 38. What arrangement of the bimetal strip do you think it will have: a flat coil or a helix? Bimetal thermometers can be made to measure temperatures in food processing and food storage (deep freeze) industries, in medical work, in the construction industry (for measuring the temperature of fluid concrete, as in Figure 19 and Figure 38, and the temperature of hot bituminous materials in roadmaking), in the mining industry, and in the petrochemical industry.

Figure 41 This shows some parts for making bimetal thermometers. The centimetre rule gives the scale. (The parts in this photograph were provided by British Rototherm, Limited, UK.)

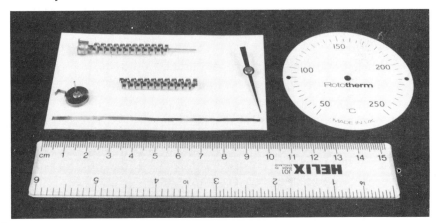

Changes of temperature and changes of properties

Very many properties of materials change when the temperatures of the materials change.

If a solid structure or component is free to move, then its **length** changes when its temperature changes. In designing machines whose temperature is going to change, the expansion and contraction of the parts has to be worked out and allowed for.

If a gas is in a container whose volume can change, then the **volume** of the gas changes when its temperature changes. When the mixture of gases in the cylinder of an engine ignites, the temperature of the gases rises; the gases expand and move the piston. This is the basis of internal combustion engines.

The **viscosity** of a liquid changes as its temperature changes. Viscosity is the property of a liquid which resists flow. Syrup and treacle do not flow easily, and have high viscosities. Water flows easily, and has a low viscosity compared with syrup. The viscosity of lubricating oils for machines is of great importance, because whether the oil will be a good lubricant or not depends mainly on its viscosity.

Machines usually start cold and run hot, so how the viscosity of a lubricating oil changes from cold starting to hot running is very

31

important. Figure 42 shows a technician measuring the viscosity of an engine oil. She is doing it with a capillary U-tube in a tank of water whose temperature can be controlled, and read with a thermometer. She can measure the viscosity of the oil at different temperatures. She can plot a graph of viscosity against temperature.

Viscosity is also very important in liquids which are used in cooling systems. The liquid must be able to flow easily around the system. Large power transformers, of about 50 kilowatts power and over, in the electricity grid are oil-cooled. Oil flows around the core and the coils, where it gets heated; and then it flows down pipes or hollow fins, which are cooled by the atmosphere. To design oil-cooled transformers, engineers need to know how the viscosity of oils changes with temperature.

Figure 43 shows graphs for two types of oils used in cooling large power transformers. The graphs show how the viscosity of the oils changes with temperature. Do the oils become more runny or less runny as the temperature rises? Which oil changes most in viscosity from −20°C to 100°C: the mineral oil or the silicone oil? (Mineral oils are made from petroleum oils.) Why do you think engineers need to know how the viscosity of oils for cooling systems change with change in temperature?

Engineers who are designing and making oil-cooled transformers also need to know how the **specific heat capacity** of cooling oils changes with temperature. The graphs in Figure 44 show this for two oils. Do the specific heat capacities increase or decrease as their temperature increases? Which specific heat capacity changes faster: the silicone oil or the mineral oil? The specific heat capacities of other materials also change with temperature.

Figure 42 The technician is measuring the viscosity of an engine oil. (Perkins Engines Limited.)

Figure 43 These graphs are for oils which are used for cooling large power transformers. The graphs show how the viscosity of each oil changes with temperature.

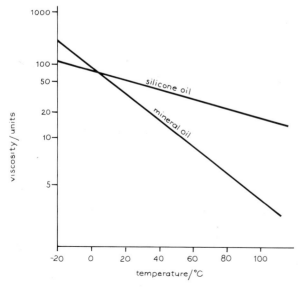

Figure 44 These graphs are for oils which are used in cooling large power transformers. The graphs show how the specific heat capacity of each oil changes with temperature.

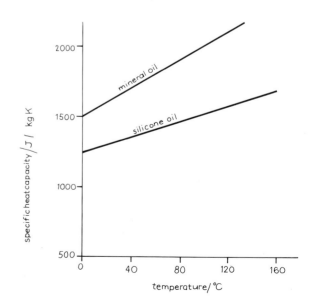

The **electrical resistance** of a conductor changes as its temperature changes. For most conductors, the resistance increases as the temperature increases. An ordinary domestic 60 W electric lamp filament has a resistance of about 80 ohms at room temperature, when the lamp is off. When the lamp is on and the filament is white-hot its resistance is about 1000 ohms. That is, when it is cold, the lamp filament has a resistance which is about $\frac{1}{12}$ of its working resistance. Does this matter?

Yes, it does matter. It can matter a great deal if a large number of lamps are switched on at once. Suppose that a string of about 20 lamps, each of 60 W power, were connected in parallel and were plugged into a 240 volt supply, as at a funfair, or a seaside promenade, or on a construction site. The total current drawn would be about 5 amps. When the lamps are switched off they cool down to atmospheric temperature, and their resistance decreases to about $\frac{1}{12}$ of the working resistance. When the lamps are switched on again, their resistance is still low, and the first surge of current is twelve times the working current, that is, $12 \times 5\,A = 60\,A$. As the lamps rapidly heat up, the resistance rapidly increases, and the current rapidly falls, to about 5 A.

Suppose that the funfair or the promenade had four strings, or festoons, of lights such as have just been described. They are switched on in the evening. What current surges through the supply just as they are switched on? What is the steady current from the supply when the lamps have all heated up? Electrical engineers have to take into account changes in resistance with changes in temperature when designing circuits and machines.

The **strength of a metal** changes and its **microscopic structure** can change as its temperature changes. Finding out about how pure metals and alloys behave at different temperatures is very important in all industries where metal components are made, and in industries where metal components are used. In some machines, the temperature of some metal parts may change repeatedly, and it is important to know how the metals stand up to the repeated changes. Figure 45 shows a technician studying the structure of a metal, using a scanning electron microscope.

Figure 45 The technician is looking at the display screens of a scanning electron microscope. She is studying the structure of a metal sample. (Perkins Engines Limited.)

33

Development Section

A Fuels and energy

Some fuels and the energy which they can give when they burn in air are described on pages 3 to 4. You should read this again.

All forms of energy are measured in joules, J. How big is a joule?

(a) If a 1 kg mass is resting on the floor and it is then lifted up through a height of 1 m, about 10 J of work have to be done.

(b) A certain block of material is resting on a table. An experiment shows that in order to push the block at a steady speed across the table against the friction, a force of 1 N is needed, pushing in the direction in which the block moves. If this 1 N force pushes the block along for 1 m across the table, then 1 J of work is done. We can therefore define the joule as follows.

If a force of 1 newton acts on a body, and if the body moves 1 metre in the direction of the force, then 1 joule of work is done.

Table 2 on page 4 shows the amount of energy that can be obtained by completely burning some fuels.

Question A.1

How many joules of energy are produced by completely burning:
(a) 2 kg of coal
(b) ½ kg of paraffin (about ¾ litre)
(c) 1 g of petrol?

A.2

How many kJ of energy are produced by completely burning:
(a) 1 kg of diesel oil
(b) 5 kg of paraffin
(c) 10 g of petrol?

B Fuels and power

When a fuel and air mixture is burned, energy is released.

Power is the rate of doing work. Power is also the rate at which energy is changed from one form into another.

$$\text{Power} = \frac{\text{work done}}{\text{time taken}} \qquad \text{Power} = \frac{\text{energy change}}{\text{time taken}}$$
$$P = W/t \qquad\qquad P = E/t$$

Because the unit of work and of energy is the joule, and the unit of time is the second, the **unit of power** is the **joule per second.**

1 joule per second = 1 watt
$$1 J/s = 1 W$$

In a low-powered hair dryer marked 500 W, the electric current does 500 J of work in the wire every second and makes the wire hot. From the hot wire, 500 J of heat are given out per second.

Calculating the power of a paraffin heater

Let us calculate the power of a large paraffin heater such as that in Figure 3, page 4. The heater burns 0.36 kg of paraffin per hour. Every 1 kg of paraffin gives out 46 000 000 J of energy when fully burned; 46 000 000 J/kg (Table 2, page 4). We need to find how many joules the heater produces per second. In one hour it gives out:

$$0.36 \text{ kg} \times 46\,000\,000 \text{ J/kg} = 0.36 \times 46\,000\,000 \text{ J}$$

So, in one second it gives out:

$$\frac{0.36 \times 46\,000\,000 \text{ J}}{60 \times 60} = 4600 \text{ J}$$

So the rate of producing energy is:

$$4600 \text{ joules per second} = 4600 \text{ W} = 4.6 \text{ kW}$$

Question B.1 Calculate the power of the following heaters, using Table 2, page 4.
(a) A large industrial space heater using 6 kg of paraffin per hour.
(b) A domestic heater using 0.2 kg of paraffin per hour.

B.2 This question is about the total power which diesel engines can produce from their fuel. Pages 5 to 6 explained that only some of the heat produced by burning fuel in an engine can be turned into work; the rest is lost as heat. Read the pages again.
   What is the power given out by the burning fuel in a diesel engine operating as follows? Use Table 2 on page 4, and give the power in kW. The engine burns diesel fuel at a rate of: (a) 6.0 kg/h, (b) 4.8 kg/h, (c) 7.2 kg/h, (d) 5.4 kg/h.
   In each case, can all of the energy which is released do work?

B.3 The engine in Question B.2. was running at the following speeds, in revolutions per minute:
(a) 2200 rev/min (b) 1800 rev/min (c) 2600 rev/min (d) 2000 rev/min
   Think of an interesting way of displaying the information in Questions B.2 and B.3. Present the data in this way. What do you notice?

C Thermal efficiencies of engines

When a fuel burns in an engine, only part of the energy produced can be turned into work. No engine can be 100% efficient; most petrol and diesel engines are between 25% and 35% efficient. This was described on pages 5 to 6, and you should read these pages.
   If the burning fuel in an engine supplies 100 000 J of energy, and if the engine does 30 000 J of useful work, then

$$\text{Efficiency} = \frac{\text{useful work got out}}{\text{total energy put in}} = \frac{30\,000 \text{ J}}{100\,000 \text{ J}} = \frac{30}{100} = 30\%$$

In another engine, the fuel supplies 80 kJ of energy per second, power = 80 kW, and the engine does 20 kJ of useful work per second, power = 20 kW.

$$\text{Efficiency} = \frac{\text{useful power got out}}{\text{total power put in}} = \frac{20\,\text{kW}}{80\,\text{kW}} = \frac{20}{80} = \frac{1}{4} = 25\%$$

Table 6   Energy supplied and work done by different engines.

	Engine	Fuel/air energy supplied	Useful work done	Efficiency
(a)	Petrol	100 kJ	22 kJ	
(b)	Diesel	100 kJ	31 kJ	
(c)	Petrol	500 kJ	100 kJ	
(d)	Diesel	900 kJ	300 kJ	
(e)	Petrol	370 MJ	85 MJ	
(f)	Diesel	753 MJ	256 MJ	

Question C.1

What is the efficiency of the engines in Table 6?

Table 7   Power measurements for the diesel engine that powers the air compressor in Figure 34, page 27, and Figure 37, page 29. The engine is made by Perkins Engines Limited UK.

Power supplied by fuel/air/kW (kJ/s)	Mechanical power of engine/kW (kJ/s)	Efficiency /%	Engine speed/rpm
54.9	16.5		1500
66.7	20.5		1800
82.6	25.6		2200
91.3	28.0		2400
99.4	30.0		2600
107.6	32.0		2800
115.8	33.5		3000

C.2

Table 7 gives data for a diesel engine.

(a) What is the power of the engine in kW at **1** 1500 rpm, **2** 3000 rpm?
(b) What is the efficiency of the engine at each of the engine speeds from 1500 rpm to 3000 rpm?
(c) Plot a graph of engine efficiency, on the y axis, against engine speed, on the x axis.
(d) What can you conclude from the graph?
(e) The air compressor in Figure 34 had its engine speed controlled by a governer, which was set at 2100 rpm. Why?

D Engines and energy balances

Where the energy goes to

Most of the energy produced by the burning fuel in a heat engine is lost, and does not do useful work. Some escapes through the exhaust, and some is carried away in the cooling system. These matters were described in 'Internal Combustion Engines and Energy', pages 3 to 6, and in 'Increasing the Loss of Heat: Cooling Systems', pages 24 to 26. You should read these pages.
    Table 8 gives information about a diesel engine.

Table 8 The table gives energy measurements on the diesel engine which powers the excavator in Figure 1. The engine is designed and made by the staff of the Ford Motor Company Ltd.

Engine speed / rpm	Fuel/air power / kw	Useful power / kw	Where the energy from the fuel goes				
			Useful work /%	Water cooling system /%	Exhaust /%	Radiation/%	Total /%
2600	191	64.7	34	16	40	10	100
1500	125	44.6	35	20	36	9	100

Question D.1 How much useful work can the engine do in 1 second at an engine speed of (a) 2600 rpm (b) 1500 rpm?

D.2 Represent a fuel tank by drawing a rectangle 100 mm high, and some suitable width. Let it represent 100 litres of fuel. Divide the rectangle up to show how 100 litres of diesel fuel are consumed at 2600 rpm. (This is done in the same way as Figure 5; and the first division would be 40 mm down to represent the exhaust losses.)

D.3 When the engine speed goes up from 1500 rpm to 2600 rpm:
(a) Does the percentage of energy lost in the engine cooling water become greater or less?
(b) Does the percentage of energy lost through the exhaust become greater or less?

Table 9 For the same engine as in Table 8, this table gives the percentage of the total power lost in the cooling water at various engine speeds.

Engine speed / rpm	1500	1800	2000	2200	2600
Cooling water power loss / % of total power	19.7	17.8	17.1	16.6	16.0

D.4 Using Table 9:
(a) Plot a graph of the % of the total power lost in the cooling water, against engine speed.
(b) Estimate the % of power lost in the cooling water at **1** 1600 rpm, **2** 2400 rpm.

Table 10 The total power from the fuel, the useful power output, and the power losses for a diesel engine running at 2500 rpm (the Ford Model 2723 engine).

Total power supplied from the fuel / kw	Useful power / kw	Cooling water loss / kw	Exhaust loss / kw	Lubricating oil loss / kw	Radiation and other losses / kw
246.3	86.6	45.6	96.2	5.4	12.5

D.5 Table 10 gives the results of experiments with a diesel engine very similar to that in Tables 8 and 9.
(a) Add up all of the figures on the right of the vertical dividing line. Compare them with the figure on the left of the line. **1** Should they agree? **2** Do they agree?
(b) What is the efficiency of the engine, as a percentage?
(c) Calculate each power loss as a percentage of the total power supplied. Arrange the losses and the engine output in order by percentages.

E Energy changes and efficiency

No practical machine is 100% efficient; some energy is always lost. Two examples were described on pages 00 to 00. Engineers have to consider costs and reliability as well as efficiency, and these ideas were also discussed. You could read the pages again.

In converting the energy of a diesel fuel/air mixture into light energy, as described on pages 00 to 00, the efficiency of each stage was this:

Stage 1 $\dfrac{30\text{J}}{100\text{J}} = 30\%$ **Stage 3** $\dfrac{2.4\text{J}}{24\text{J}} = \dfrac{1}{10} = 10\%$

Stage 2 $\dfrac{24\text{J}}{30\text{J}} = \dfrac{8}{10} = 80\%$

The overall efficiency can be found by multiplying together all the individual efficiencies.

$$\text{Overall efficiency} = \frac{30}{100} \times \frac{80}{100} \times \frac{10}{100} = \frac{2.4}{100} = 2.4\%$$

Is this the same figure that was obtained on page 00?

Question E.1

Find the overall efficiency of the following systems:
(a) A diesel engine burns fuel, and does work with 30% efficiency. The engine drives a water pump which is 40% efficient.
(b) A petrol engine burns fuel and does work with 20% efficiency. The engine drives an alternator which produces alternating current with 70% efficiency.
(c) A diesel engine burns fuel, does work with an efficiency of 30%, and drives an alternator which is 90% efficient.

Finding what engine power to order

Engineers who design and make equipment such as pumps for pumping water out of excavations need to arrange for the equipment to be provided with a suitable engine. The engine must provide the power that will be needed.

A pump has been designed to deliver up to 5.0 kW of power to water. The pump is 20% efficient. How much power will the engine have to provide to the pump?

$$\text{Efficiency} = \frac{\text{Useful power got out}}{\text{Total power put in}}$$

$$20\% = \frac{5.0\,\text{kW}}{\text{Total power put in}}$$

$$\text{Total power put in} = \frac{5.0\,\text{kW}}{20\%} = \frac{5.0\,\text{kW}}{20/100} = \frac{5.0\,\text{kW} \times 100}{20}$$

$$= 5\,\text{kW} \times 5 = 25\,\text{kW}$$

Therefore the engine must provide at least 25 kW to the pump.

E.2 Find what power of engine is needed for the following equipment:
(a) A water pump which is to deliver up to 10 kW of power to water; the pump is 25% efficient.
(b) An alternator which is to produce up to 16 kW of electric power; the alternator is 80% efficient.

Table 11 Some materials, and the changes in length which occur when a 10 m length (10000 mm) of material has its temperature changed through 10 K.

Material	Change in length / mm	Material	Change in length / mm
Aluminium	2.4	Concrete	1.2
Brass	2.0	Glass (window)	0.8
Copper	1.7	Brick	0.6
Iron	1.2	Invar (an alloy)	0.1
Steel	1.2	Vitreous silica	0.05

F Thermal expansion and contraction

Most materials expand when their temperatures are raised, and they contract when their temperatures are lowered. Different materials expand and contract to different extents, when compared with each other. If a bar of aluminium is 10 m long and is cooled through a temperature difference of 10 K, its length decreases by 2.4 mm. If a bar or iron is also 10 m long and it, too, is cooled through a temperature difference of 10 K, its length decreases by 1.2 mm. This is only half of the change in the aluminium bar.

Usually the change in length is proportional to the change in temperature, so a bar of brass 10 m long, when heated through a temperature difference of 20 K, will expand by twice the length that a 10 K change will produce. It will expand by 4.0 mm, instead of 2.0 mm.

Most machines and structures heat up and cool down, so most machines and structures expand and contract. In a machine, different parts may have to be made with different materials; and as the machine heats up these parts will expand to different extents. Engineers need to design and to make machines in ways that will allow for this.

You should read "Explanation and Contraction", pages 16 to 19. For questions F.1 to F.7 you can use the data in Table 11.

Question F.1 Ten-metre long bars of the following materials have their temperature raised from 20 °C to 30 °C. How many mm does each expand?
(a) Copper   (b) Concrete   (c) Glass

F.2 Twenty-metre long rods of the following materials have their temperature raised from 20 °C to 30 °C. How many mm does each expand?
(a) Aluminium   (b) Steel   (c) Invar

F.3 Ten-metre long bars of the following materials have their temperatures lowered from 60 °C to 30 °C. How many mm does each contract?
(a) Brass   (b) Concrete

F.4 Twenty-metre long rods of the following materials have their temperature raised from 10°C to 40°C. How many mm does each expand?
(a) Iron   (b) Brass

F.5 A bridge beam is made of reinforced concrete, that is, concrete with steel rods in it. The beam is 30 m long. One cold winter its temperature was −10°C, and in the hottest part of the following summer its temperature was 20°C.
(a) How much did its temperature change?
(b) How much did its length change?

F.6 In a district heating system, the distance from the main boilerhouse to a building which uses the hot water is 200 m. The hot water is supplied under pressure, at 110°C. Suppose that a straight steel pipe was laid, at a temperature of 10°C, to connect the boilerhouse to the building; and suppose the hot water was then passed down the pipe.
(a) If the pipe was free to move at one end because it had a flexible connection, by how much would its length change?
(b) If the pipe was laid with normal fixed connections at each end, what might happen?
(c) What arrangement could be used to prevent damage?

F.7 Reinforced concrete is a very important constructional material. To make it, steel rods are placed in precise positions in a mould of the shape needed. Fluid concrete is poured into the mould. The concrete flows round the rods and takes up the shape of the mould. As the concrete sets, the steel and the concrete form strong chemical bonds between each other. They become strongly attached to each other.
(a) From Table 11, what do you notice about the extent to which steel expands and contracts, and concrete expands and contracts under the same conditions?
(b) Do you think that this would cause any great strain on the bonds between the steel and the concrete?
(c) If aluminium rods had been used to reinforce the concrete, do you think temperature changes would set up strains in bonds between the aluminium and the concrete?
(d) If so, what might happen to the concrete after repeated expansions and contractions?

G   Heat transfer

How heat can be transferred from one place to another is very important to all engineers.

In an electric motor and in an electric generator, currents flow in the windings. These currents raise the temperature of the windings. If the temperature becomes too high, the electrical insulation will be damaged. Motors and generators must be designed and manufactured so that the heat is removed fast enough to avoid this. Therefore, electrical engineers need to know how heat can be transferred.

Combustion engines burn a mixture of air and a fuel, such as petrol, kerosine or diesel fuel, and the flame temperatures are very high: often about 2000°C. Of the energy in the fuel and air mixture, only about 20% to 35% will be changed into useful energy; the rest, 80% to 65%, has to be removed from the engine. Mechanical engineers who design and make internal combustion engines need to know how heat travels from a combustion chamber through the metal walls to the outer surface; and they need to know how to remove it from the outer surface, perhaps by water cooling or by air cooling.

Some engineers are interested in keeping machines and buildings warm, and in preventing heat from being transferred. They need to know how insulators behave.

How heat travels

When heat travels from one place to another place it always travels **from** the place at the **higher** temperature **to** the place at the **lower** temperature.

The heat travels by three main methods:
conduction, convection and **radiation**.

Conduction

Conduction can take place in solids, liquids and gases. The particles pass energy from one to another by **vibrations** and by **collisions**. In solids, the atoms or molecules or ions vibrate about an average position; and this average position is fixed in the structure.

In liquids or gases, the molecules and ions are free to move about; and they can change their positions relative to each other.

The best particles for carrying heat are electrons. In metals there are large numbers of free electrons, and they are able to move about in the lattice structure carrying energy with them. Therefore, metals are good conductors of heat. Electrons also carry electric currents, so metals are good conductors of electricity, too.

Table 12 The relative heat conductivities of some materials.

Material	Relative heat conductivity	Material	Relative heat conductivity	
		Boiler scale (variable)	0.9	
Silver	420	Water	0.7	
Copper	380	Plywood	0.2	
Aluminium (pure)	200	PVC (Polyvinylchloride)	0.15	
Aluminium alloy	100	Timber	0.1	
		Motor oil (motionless)	0.1	*BAD*
Iron (cast iron)	75	Cork	0.05	*CONDUCTORS*
Steel	60	Rockwool	0.04	*and*
Carbon, graphite (very variable)	5 to 0.05			*therefore*
Concrete	1.5	Glass wool	0.04	*GOOD*
Brick	1.0	Air (motionless)	0.02	*INSULATORS*
Glass	1.0			

An engineer who is designing a heat transfer system needs to know how much heat will be conducted through a material of a particular thickness and some particular area per second. Measurements have been done on a very large number of different materials to find this information.

We can draw interesting comparisons between the electrical conductivity and the heat conductivity of materials, as shown in Table 13.

Table 13   Some materials, and their electrical and thermal properties.

Material	Electrical conductivity	Electrical use	Thermal conductivity	Thermal use
Copper	Very high	Wires and cables	Very high	Heat exchangers
Aluminium	Very high	Wires and cables	Very high	Heat exchangers
Glass	Very low	Insulators on power lines	Low	Glass wool insulation (but see Air, below)
PVC	Very low	Insulation for wires and cables	Low	
Air	Very low	Insulation	Very low	Insulation; especially in 'wool' and plastic foam form.

The reason why glass wool makes very good insulation is not that glass is a poor thermal conductor; it is that air is a very bad conductor. The glass fibres trap very small pockets of air, and this air is unable to move. The very bad conductivity of the still air makes excellent insulation. This applies also to other 'wool' products such as 'Rockwool'. Both 'Rockwool' and glass wool are used for insulating houses in the roof spaces and the cavity walls. Figure 28 on page 20 shows a Rockwool unit in a cavity wall under construction. Read the section 'Reducing the loss of heat: Insulation', pages 19 to 24.

Questions on heat losses from buildings
For Questions G.1 to G.5 you should use the data in Figure 30, page 21. This shows the heat loss through $1\,m^2$ areas of various structures if there is a temperature difference of 10 K between one side and the other.

Question G.1 A window measures 1½ m × 2 m. The temperature inside the room is 20 °C and the temperature outside the window is 10 °C.
(a) What is the rate at which heat is being lost through the window, in W?
(b) How many J/s is this?

G.2 During the night, the temperature outside the house in Question G.1 drops to 0 °C. The room remains at 20 °C. What is the rate of loss of heat through the window?

G.3 The room in Question G.1. has a door which leads outside. The door measures 2 m × ¾ m. What is the rate of heat loss through the door?

G.4 A room has an outside wall with no windows. The wall is of simple cavity construction, as in Figure 30(c), and it measures 4 m × 2½ m. The temperature inside the room is 10 °C and that outside is 0 °C.
(a) What is the rate of heat loss through the walls?
(b) In the evening the central heating goes on, and the inside temperature rises to 20 °C. What is the evening rate of heat loss?

G.5 The owner of the house in Question G.4 has the wall cavity filled with insulation. What will the new rates of heat loss be for the temperatures in Question G.4?

Diesel engine heat transfer

How much heat passes per second through the cylinder walls of a diesel engine? Have a look at Figure 37, page 29; this shows an air compressor. It is driven by a diesel engine, which is above the wheel. The engine can provide 30 kW of power to the compressor; and while this is being done, 22 kW of heat are carried away from the cylinder walls by the water cooling system. Have a look at Figure 4, page 4; this shows the piston, cylinder, and water-jacket of an internal combustion engine. (It is actually a spark ignition engine; a diesel engine would have a very similar design and no spark plug.)

Heat from the explosion and flame in the cylinder is conducted through the cast-iron wall of the cylinder and into the water which surrounds the cylinder.

We can make an approximate calculation of how much heat passes through 1 cm² of cylinder wall per second. In the air compressor's diesel engine the circumference of each cylinder is 25 cm; and the length of cylinder which is in contact with cooling water is approximately 11 cm. If you imagine the cylinder wall to be cut down one side and then unrolled, it would form a rectangle 25 cm × 11 cm. Therefore, the area of each cylinder wall is 25 cm × 11 cm. There are four cylinders.

Total area of cylinder walls = 4 × 25 cm × 11 cm = 1100 cm²

Twenty-two kilowatts of power pass through this area of wall to the cooling water. Therefore,

$$\text{Power passing through } 1\,\text{cm}^2 = \frac{22\,000\,\text{W}}{1100\,\text{cm}^2} = 20\,\text{W/cm}^2$$

20 W is 20 J/s. Now 20 J of energy will lift a 2 kg mass vertically upwards through 1 m. Every second this amount of energy flows through 1 cm² of cylinder wall.

The cylinder walls of a new engine will be clean; but as the engine runs, thin films of deposits form on the walls. Incomplete burning of the fuel in the upper part of the cylinder results in a deposit of very fine particles of carbon; lubrication in the lower part of the cylinder results in a thin film of oil, as shown in Figure 46. On the cooling water side, impurities in the water will lead to the formation of scale deposits; and outside that there is a thin layer of stationary water.

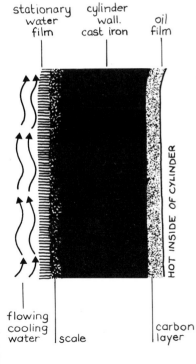

Figure 46 This is a cross-section of the cylinder wall of a petrol or diesel engine. The diagram is enlarged.

stationary water film   cylinder wall. cast iron   oil film

HOT INSIDE OF CYLINDER

flowing cooling water   scale   carbon layer

G.6 (a) Draw a sketch of a cross-section of an engine cylinder wall with its layers.

(b) Using Table 12, label the layers with the relative heat conductivity values for oil, carbon, cast iron, scale and stationary water.

(c) Compared with a clean metal cylinder wall, will the working wall with its layers be the same, better or worse as a conductor?

(d) As the layers form, will the flow of heat from the explosions to the cooling water speed up, slow down or remain the same?

(e) Will the temperature in the cylinder rise, fall or stay the same?

G.7 The following is an extract from the Installation Manual of a diesel engine manufacturer, but for this question part of a sentence has been left out.

Coolant Water Quality. The use of soft water is desirable because

_____

_____

The quality of the water used should if possible meet the following requirements:

pH	6.5–8.0	Sulphate concentration	max. 0.01%
Chloride concentration max. 0.01%		Hardness (total)	max. 0.03%

Assume that you are the writer of the Manual for customers. Write a full first sentence. Also explain what pH 6.5–8.0 means; and describe how the pH of the water could be found. (Extracted from General Installation Manual, Perkins Engines Ltd.)

Convection

Heat transfer by convection occurs in liquids and gases. Large-scale movement of the liquid or gas takes place. In **natural convection** the movement is caused by **density changes** in the liquid or gas. A liquid which is being warmed expands and its density becomes lower; this liquid can then float upwards through colder, denser liquid.

In **forced convection** the movement of the liquid or gas is **produced mechanically**. For instance, a fan may be used to draw air over the hot parts of a machine; or an impeller may be used to force a liquid round a cooling system.

Natural convection and forced convection are both important in engineering. The ways in which density changes produce a **convection current** in the cooling system of a water-cooled engine were described on pages 24 to 26, 'Increasing the loss of heat: cooling systems'. You should read this section.

Radiation

All bodies which are above the absolute zero of temperature emit electromagnetic radiation. **Electromagnetic radiation carries energy with it.** If a body absorbs electromagnetic radiation and its energy, then the temperature of the body rises.

The higher the temperature of a body, the more radiation energy it emits per m^2 of its surface.

The **type of surface** which a body has affects how the body behaves with electromagnetic radiation. A **black surface** is a **good**

Figure 47 Panels with shiny aluminium foil are being fixed to the inside of a cavity wall. The shiny surface will reduce heat loss by radiation.

emitter and a **good absorber** of radiation. A highly polished metal surface is a **bad emitter** and a **bad absorber** of radiation; because it is a bad absorber it is a **good reflector**.

Electromagnetic radiation can travel through a vacuum.

In Figure 47, the panels at the bottom right of the building are reflecting sunlight, and they are reflecting an image of the ladder and the panel fixer. The panels are on the inside wall of what will be a cavity wall. The reflecting surface is aluminium foil, and it faces **outwards** from the building. It is a good reflector, and it is a **bad radiator**. Putting the aluminium foil on the wall reduces the radiant heat loss from the building, because the shiny surface is a bad radiator.

Many buildings are now constructed with shiny aluminium foil on the inner wall, to reduce heat loss by radiation. The foil also acts as a moisture barrier.

In Table 14, a perfect radiator would have a relative value of 1.0. Lampblack (very pure soot) is one of the most efficient radiators. The lower the relative value, the poorer is the material as a radiator. Polished copper is a very bad radiator.

Table 14   Some materials, and their relative effectiveness as radiators of electromagnetic radiation.

Material	Relative effectiveness as a radiator
Copper (a) polished	0.02
(b) oxidised (with a black copper oxide surface)	0.6
Aluminium, polished	0.04
Steel (a) polished	0.07
(b) oxidized (rusty)	0.8
Tungsten, lamp filament	0.3
Building brick	0.9
Lampblack (soot) paint	0.96
A perfect radiator	1.0

G.8 **Table 15** Table 15 lists four materials. On notepaper, make a similar Table. Describe the properties of the materials as radiators, absorbers, and reflectors of radiation. Use the words Very good, Quite good, Medium, Poor, Very bad; and fill in the columns in your Table.

Material	Radiator	Absorber	Reflector
Polished aluminium			
Copper with a coating of black copper oxide			
Building brick			
A lamp filament of tungsten			

Radiation in diesel engines

When the fuel and air mixture in the cylinder burns, carbon particles are formed and these become hot. They emit radiation, and this radiation carries about 10% of the energy that goes to the cylinder walls as heat.

The main function of the oil in an engine is to lubricate the moving parts. It also helps in the cooling of some parts as it circulates around the engine.

Figure 48 shows the oil circulation in simple form. Relatively cool oil is pumped from the sump up to the top of the engine, and to other parts. It runs down through the hot engine and may reach a temperature of about 110°C. It then drains into the sump, where heat is given off mainly by radiation. This reduces the temperature, and the oil in the sump may be at about 70°C or 80°C.

About 3% of the total cooling may be done by the oil. Another 7% or so occurs by radiation from other surfaces of the engine, so radiation contributes a total of about 10% of the cooling.

Figure 48 The engine oil is being cooled mainly by radiation from the sump case. (Adapted from General Installation Manual, Perkins Engines Limited, UK.)

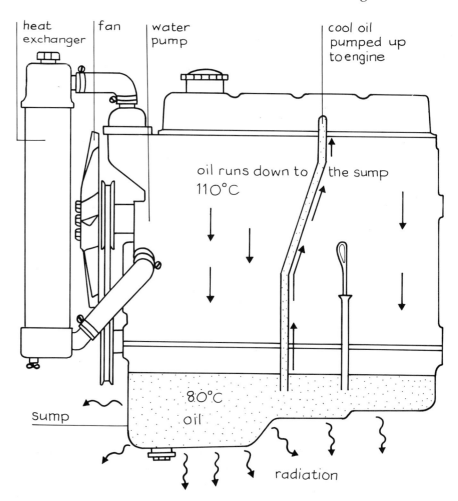

Figure 49 This is a tungsten halogen floodlight. It is designed and made by staff at Crompton Parkinson Ltd, UK.

A tungsten halogen floodlight

Figure 6 shows a telescopic lighting mast on a trailer, with four 1000 W floodlights on top of the mast. Figure 49 shows a similar floodlight; it uses 500 W of electrical power, and measures 20 cm across the front by 15 cm down the front.

The lamp is a straight tube made from silica, and the filament is of high purity tungsten. Inside the lamp are a little nitrogen, argon and iodine at low pressure. Tungsten halogen lamps are used on construction sites and elsewhere because they are sturdy, and they survive jolts and knocks much better than ordinary tungsten filament lamps. They have a life which is twice as long as that of an ordinary filament lamp; and they are simple and cheap to manufacture.

When the lamp is working, the temperature of the filament is about 2750 °C, and the temperature of the silica tube is about 750 °C.

G.9 (a) From Figure 49, draw a sketch which gives a cross-section of the floodlight. The curved, parabola-shaped mirror touches the main body at the front and at the back; elsewhere there is an air gap between the mirror and the body. The fins go down the back of the body and underneath it.

(b) Mark in the temperatures of **1** the filament, 2750 °C **2** the lamp tube, 750 °C **3** the air inside the main body space, 300 °C **4** the outside of the glass front, 150 °C **5** the outside of the case, and the roots of the fins, 65 °C.

(c) Energy is given to the floodlight by the electric current. Mark in the ways in which it leaves **1** through the glass front: 10% by visible radiation, and 50% by infra-red radiation **2** from the body: 10% by radiation (infra-red) **3** from the glass front and from the body: 30% by convection. Add up the percentages, as a check.

(d) Sketch in some arrows to show air convection currents flowing past the glass front.

(e) Do the same for the body and fins.

(f) Suppose that the temperature of the atmosphere is 15 °C. Make an estimate of the sort of temperature that the air might have: **1** just below and in front of the glass cover **2** just above and in front of the glass cover **3** just below a fin at the bottom **4** just above a fin at the top.

(g) A floodlight consumes 1000 W of electrical power. Use the data in (c) to calculate **1** How many watts of visible light it emits **2** How much power is removed from the lamp by convection.

Conduction, convection and radiation together

In most practical situations, heat is lost by a combination of conduction, convection and radiation.

G.10 Examine closely the floodlight in Figure 49. By what route could heat from the white-hot filament be lost by conduction?

G.11 (a) Make a full-page drawing to show the main ways in which the heat from the explosions in a diesel engine cylinder leaves the engine. You can combine the features of Figure 4 and Figure 48.

47

(b) Starting with the flame from the burning fuel in the cylinder, describe the ways in which heat is transferred from the inside of the cylinder to the outside atmosphere. Label your diagram suitably at each stage: radiation, conduction, natural convection, or forced convection.

H Electricity and heat

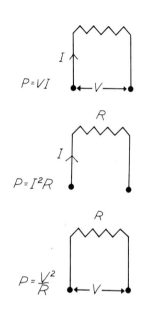

$$P = VI$$

$$P = I^2R$$

$$P = \frac{V^2}{R}$$

Figure 50 The rate at which heat is produced in electric circuits.

An electric current in a conductor raises the temperature of the conductor. This is obvious in an electric light bulb, which becomes very hot to touch; and it is obvious in an electric convector heater. It may not be so obvious in an electric power cable, though it still happens there. It also occurs in the wire windings of the coils which are needed in electromagnetic machinery, such as electric motors, generators, transformers, relays and solenoids. When an engineer is designing equipment of this sort, one of the first needs is to work out how much heat will be produced in the machine and how it can be removed. If the heat is not removed fast enough the temperature of the equipment will rise, and the insulation could become damaged or destroyed. Then the windings will become damaged or destroyed.

In an electric generator, cooling air must be drawn over the coils; in a transformer, the coils must be cooled by oil or by air. Engineers therefore need to know the rate at which heat will be produced by an electric circuit, or by a part of it. Figure 50, shows how this may be calculated.

If we use volts, amps, and ohms to substitute for V, I and R, each equation gives the heat produced in its circuit per second, as joules per second. This is a rate of change of energy and is therefore power, and it is measured in watts.

$$1\,\text{J/s} = 1\,\text{W}$$

H.1 Relay coils and heat production

Figure 51 shows an industrial relay. A coil of wire surrounds a magnetically soft steel core; this electromagnet can attract the soft steel on the moveable arm, or armature, on the left. The manufacturer makes a range of relays, and some of the data for them is shown in Table 16.

Find in watts the rate at which heat is produced by each coil, A, B, C and D.

This quantity of heat per second can easily escape from the coil, and no special cooling arrangement is needed.

Table 16 Coil data for relays.

Relay	Voltage/V	Current/A	Working resistance/Ω
A	6	0.4	—
B	12	0.1	—
C	6	—	30
D	12	—	120

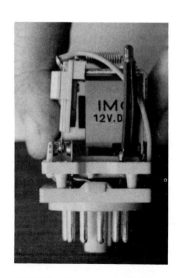

Figure 51 This is an industrial relay.

H.2 Cables and heat losses

Figure 52 The engineer is examining a mains cable on a site. The cable contains four conductors each able to carry a current of 185A.

(a) In the cable in Figure 52, the resistance of a live conductor and a neutral conductor together are: for a 125m length of cable, 0.2Ω; and for a 250m length of cable 0.4Ω. What is the power loss as heat:

1 if the cable is 125m long and carries a current of 50A?

2 If the cable is 250m long and carries a current of 30A?

(b) A much thicker cable than that in Figure 52 has conductors which may carry a current of 310A. The resistance of a live conductor and a neutral conductor together are: for 330m of cable, 0.1Ω; and for 660m of cable, 0.2Ω. What is the power loss as heat:

1 If the cable is 330m long and carries 100A?

2 If the cable is 660m long and carries 80A?

(c) The temperature of the conductors could rise to a value at which the insulation would begin to become soft. The manufacturer has therefore recommended maximum current values, of 185A for the cable in (a) and 310A for the cable in (b), provided that the cables are in the open. If they are indoors and surrounded by a metal 'trunking', then lower current values are recommended. Why do you think this is?

H.3 Transformers and energy losses.

(a) A small, portable transformer has a maximum output of 5kW of power. For one job it was being used at about 90% of full power, and the primary and secondary currents are shown in Table 17.

Table 17 This gives the coil resistances and coil currents in a small transformer (maximum power output, 5kW).

Coil	Resistance	Current
Primary	0.42 Ω	61.7 A
Secondary	0.0011 Ω	1000 A

Calculate the rate at which heat is being produced in **1** the primary coil, and **2** the secondary coil.

Other sources of heat in the transformer produce a further 90W. If the transformer is placed in a steel box, the heat can escape fast enough to avoid overheating, and no special cooling arrangements are needed.

(b) A large power transformer can deliver 500kW. For a period of time it was being used at about 80% of full power, and the primary and secondary currents are shown in Table 18.

Table 18 This gives the coil resistances and coil currents in a large power transformer (maximum power output, 500kW).

Coil	Resistance	Current
Primary	0.212 Ω	10 A
Secondary	0.013 Ω	38.7 A

Calculate the rate at which heat is being produced in **1** the secondary coil, and **2** the primary coil.

These rates of heat production are so great that the transformer has to be placed in a tank of oil, with cooling fins on the tank. In addition to the heat calculated in **1** and **2**, other sources produce about a further 4kW.

I Boiling temperature and pressure

The temperature at which a liquid boils depends upon the pressure on the liquid. If the pressure increases, the boiling temperature increases; if the pressure decreases, the boiling temperature decreases. Water at 1 atmosphere pressure boils at 100°C; but at the higher pressure of 2 atmospheres it boils at about 120°C, and at the reduced pressure of ½ atmosphere it boils at about 80°C.

This effect can be useful and it can be a nuisance. It is useful in pressure cookers, and in producing superheated water and steam for heating purposes. An example of the latter was described on page 16 under 'Expansion and Contraction'.

The effect can be a nuisance when water-cooled engines are used at heights over 500 m above sea level. The greater the height of a place, the less is the pressure of the atmosphere at that place. An engine whose water cooling system ran very satisfactorily at 92°C at sea level would boil at a height of 3000 m. Figure 53 shows how the boiling temperature of water decreases as height increases.

A convenient and relatively simple answer to the problem is to fit a steam-tight pressure cap to the radiator filler. Then the pressure inside the water system can be above that of the atmosphere outside. A common excess pressure is 28 kPa, about ¼ atmosphere. Figure 53 shows how the boiling point of water in a pressurized radiator changes with altitude.

Figure 53 This shows how the boiling temperature of water changes with height above sea level.

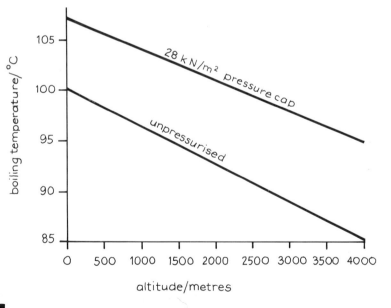

altitude/metres

Question I.1

(a) At what temperature does water boil in an open vessel, or in an unsealed radiator of an engine, when it is at the following altitudes above sea level: **1** 0 m **2** 1000 m **3** 3000 m?

(b) An engine has a water-cooled radiator with a pressure cap which allows the steam to reach a pressure of 28 kPa above the pressure of the outside atmosphere. At what temperatures will the water in the radiator boil at altitudes of **1** 0 m **2** 1000 m **3** 3000 m?

I.2 A manufacturer of water-cooled diesel engines writes in the Manual, 'In order to allow for the possibility of faulty setting of the pressure cap, the maximum temperature of the water at the engine outlet (to the radiator) must not rise closer to the boiling temperature of water than 8 °C.'
(Adapted from General Installation Manual, Perkins Engines Limited, UK.)
   With a 28 kPa pressure cap, what is the maximum allowable temperature of the water at the engine outlet (a) at 2000 m (b) at 3500 m?

I.3 The diesel engine Manual in Question I.2 later states 'Experience has shown that pressure caps should not be set to provide an excess pressure of more than 90 kPa above the atmosphere outside.
The reasons are _____
   Write two or three sentences to complete this section of the Manual (90 kPa is almost equal to 1 atmosphere pressure, 101 kPa). You might like to consider: the pressure outside the cooling system; the pressure inside the cooling system; and the effect of this on such parts of the system as hoses, hose joints, seals, and gaskets. (Adapted from General Installation Manual, Perkins Engines Limited, UK.)

J Heat capacity

Energy has to be supplied to a body to raise its temperature. The heat which has to be supplied to a body to raise its temperature through 1 K is called the **heat capacity of the body**. It is measured in joules per kelvin, J/K.

A lump of concrete required 3000 J to raise its temperature from 12 °C to 13 °C. The heat capacity of the lump is 3000 J/K.

The heat which has to be supplied to 1 kg of a substance to raise the temperature of it through 1 K is called the specific heat capacity, C, of the substance. It is measured in joules per kilogram kelvin, J/kg K.

If the mass of the lump of concrete referred to was 3 kg, then its specific heat capacity is

$$\frac{3000\,\text{J/K}}{3\,\text{kg}} = 1000\,\text{J/kg K}$$

The amount of heat needed to raise 1 kg of water through 1 K is 4200 J.

Table 19 The specific heat capacities of some materials.

Substance	Specific heat capacity, C (J/kg K)	Substance	Specific heat capacity, C (J/kg K)
Water	4200	Aluminium (alloy)	880
Ice	2100	Brick (varies)	840
Paraffin oil	2100	Glass (varies)	700
Motor oil	1600	Iron	450
Air	1000	Steel (varies)	420
Concrete (varies)	1000	Copper	390
Aluminium (pure)	900	Zinc	390

The amount of heat, Q, needed to raise 2 kg of water from 10°C to 13°C is:

$$Q = 2\,kg \times 4200\,J/kg\,K \times 3\,K$$
$$= 2 \quad \times 4200\,J \qquad \times 3$$
$$= 25\,200\,J$$

The general equation is $Q = mC\,(\theta_2 - \theta_1)$.
m, mass; C, specific heat capacity; θ_1 and θ_2, temperatures.

Questions J.1–J.5

For these questions use the data in Table 19. One metre³ of air has a mass of 1.3 kg. One litre of water has a mass of 1 kg.

J.1
(a) An engine contains 10 kg of oil. How much heat is needed to raise the oil from a starting temperature of 10°C to the average running temperature of 100°C?
(b) An engine water cooling system contains 20 kg of water. How much heat is needed to raise the water from a starting temperature of 10°C to the average running temperature of 90°C?
(c) An engine contains 7 kg of oil, and the average running temperature of the oil is 95°C. The engine is switched off, and the oil cools to 15°C. How much heat is given out?
(d) An engine cooling system contains 30 kg of water. The engine is switched off, and the water cools from its average running temperature of 93°C to atmospheric temperature of 23°C. How much heat is given out?

J.2
Look at Figure 32, page 23. The site office measures 9 m long by 3 m wide by 2 m high. It is divided into two rooms and these have to be heated.
(a) One room is 5 m × 3 m × 2 m. The air in it is warmed from 2°C to 22°C. How much heat is needed?
(b) The other room is 4 m × 3 m × 2 m, and the air is raised from 2°C to 12°C. How much heat is needed?

J.3
Water cooling of engines
Look at Figure 33, page 24 and Figure 48, page 46, which show parts of water cooling systems for engines. Table 20 gives the performance of some engine cooling systems, each having a fan and water pump. Work out the performance of the cooling systems and complete the two righthand columns.

Table 20 The performance of some water-cooled heat exchangers.

	Water flow rate	Temperature at top of heat exchanger	Temperature at bottom of heat exchanger	Heat removed	Power removed / kW
(a)	1 kg/s	90 °C	85 °C	kJ/s	
(b)	1 kg/s	92 °C	86 °C	kJ/s	
(c)	120 kg/min	99 °C	93 °C	kJ/min	
(d)	90 kg/min	98 °C	93 °C	kJ/min	

J.4 | **Ventilation of rooms**

The construction industry's guide for occupied rooms recommends the following complete air changes per hour: large shops, ½; offices, 1; school classrooms, 2.

(a) The site office in Figure 31, page 22 measures 9m × 3m × 2m; on a winter day the temperature of the air outside is −5°C, and inside it is 25°C. Calculate the power needed to give one complete air change per hour, through windows which are open the right amount.

J.5 | **Air cooling of machinery**

(a) Figure 2, page 3 shows a water pump which is driven by a one-cylinder air-cooled diesel engine. The engine output of power along the shaft is 5kW. Cooling air is to be blown over the finned engine so that 10kW of power is removed by the air. The rise in air temperature must be kept to a maximum of 40K. At what rate will air have to be blown over the engine **1** in m³/s **2** in m³/min. Use Table 19.

(b) A portable a.c. generator mounted on a trolley produces 5kW of electric power. The current in the coils and other causes generate 1.2kW of power as heat. Air has to be drawn through the machine to keep it cool. The temperature of the air must not rise more than 30K. What rate of air flow will be needed **1** in m³/s **2** in m³/min? Use Table 19.

K The Gas Laws

Engineers who design and make internal combustion engines, gas turbines and other heat engines, or who design and make gas compressors, spend a great deal of their time using the gas laws. In order to make a good design, they must know how gases are going to behave when their volume is changed, or their temperature is changed, or their pressure is changed.

In simple gas changes there are **four quantities** that might change. They are the **mass, pressure, volume** and **temperature** of the gas.

Figure 54 This shows a piston trapping some gas in a cylinder. The graph shows how the pressure in the trapped gas changes with its volume.

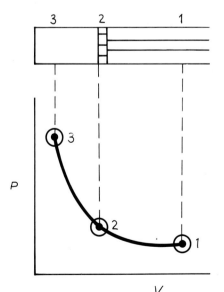

Figure 55 This shows how the volume of a fixed mass of gas changes with its temperature.

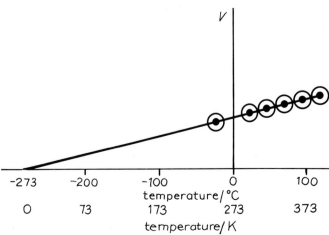

Boyle's Law

Figure 54 shows some gas trapped in a cylinder by a moveable piston. The mass of gas is fixed. If the temperature is kept constant, and if the volume is decreased, then the pressure is increased. Measurements show that if the volume is halved then the pressure becomes doubled. If the volume is reduced to $\frac{1}{5}$ of the original, the pressure rises to 5 times the original.

The pressure of the gas is inversely proportional to its volume, when mass and temperature are constant.

$$p \propto \frac{1}{V}$$

If we take corresponding values of p and V, and multiply them, we find that $p \times V$ = a constant.

Each corresponding pair of readings, when multiplied together, equals this constant, so

$p_1 V_1 = C$ and $p_2 V_2 = C$

Therefore $p_1 V_1 = p_2 V_2$

The Volume Law

Figure 55 shows a graph of how the volume of a fixed mass of gas changes as its temperature is changed, when the pressure is kept constant.

The volume of the gas is directly proportional to its absolute temperature, on the kelvin scale of temperature, when mass and pressure are constant.

$V \propto T$ (mass and pressure being constant)

The Pressure Law

The pressure of a fixed mass of gas is directly proportional to its absolute temperature, if its volume is kept constant.

$p \propto T$ (mass and volume being constant)

Kelvin temperatures and celsius temperatures

It matters a very great deal whether we use kelvin temperatures or celsius temperatures in calculations on gases, and so in calculations on engines. A scale which starts with its zero at the absolute zero of temperature is needed, and this is the kelvin scale (see Figure 55).

Engineers also use the kelvin scale for working out the theoretical efficiency of a heat engine. If the engine is getting its energy from a source which is at a high temperature T_{high}, and if the exhaust gases are going into the atmosphere at a temperature

T_{low}, then the maximum efficiency which the engine can theoretically have is

$$\text{Efficiency} = 1 - \frac{T_{low}}{T_{high}}$$

This equation comes from work done by a French engineer called Carnot and the Scottish engineer Lord Kelvin. The kelvin scale of temperature is called after Lord Kelvin.

The temperatures must be measured from the absolute zero of temperature, so they must be kelvin temperatures.

Let us find the maximum theoretical efficiency of a heat engine which is working in the atmosphere at a temperature of 27°C, and which is getting its heat from a source at a temperature of 927°C.

$$T_{low} = 27°C = (273 + 27)K = 300\,K$$

So the atmospheric temperature is 300 K.

$$T_{high} = 927°C = (273 + 927)K = 1200\,K$$

So the source of heat is at a temperature of 1200 K.

$$\text{Efficiency} = 1 - \frac{T_{low}}{T_{high}}$$

$$= 1 - \frac{300\,K}{1200\,K} = 1 - \frac{3}{12} = 1 - \frac{1}{4} = \frac{3}{4} = 75\%$$

Therefore, the maximum theoretical efficiency of the engine is 75%. In practice, engines only achieve about half of the theoretical efficiency or less, so this engine would probably be only about 30% to 35% efficient.

The equation of Carnot and Kelvin guides engineers, and its temperatures are absolute temperatures measured in kelvin.

Celsius and kelvin temperatures

The relationship between celsius temperatures and kelvin temperatures is shown in Figure 55.

celsius temperature /°C = kelvin temperature/K − 273

Question K.1 Convert the following celsius temperatures into kelvin temperatures:
(a) 0°C (b) 7°C (c) 17°C (d) 50°C (e) 100°C (f) 200°C
(g) 260°C (h) 1000°C (i) 2700°C

K.2 Convert the following celsius temperatures into kelvin temperatures:
(a) −3°C (b) −10°C (c) −31°C (d) −150°C (e) −222°C
(f) − 273°C

K.3 Convert the following kelvin temperatures into celsius temperatures:
(a) 273K (b) 283K (c) 298K (d) 373K (e) 395K (f) 600K
(g) 1373K (h) 2500K

K.4 Convert the following kelvin temperatures into celsius temperatures:
(a) 270 K (b) 260 K (c) 242 K (d) 150 K (e) 91 K (f) 10 K (g) 0 K

Kelvin temperatures and the efficiency of heat engines

K.5 The equation which is used to calculate the highest theoretical efficiency of heat engines was given on page 54. Read about this again, and use the equation to find the highest theoretical efficiency of the following heat engines.
(a) The engine is working in an atmosphere at 27 °C; and the source of heat is at 127 °C.
(b) The atmosphere is at 27 °C, and the source of heat is at 327 °C.
(c) The atmosphere is at 27 °C, and the source of heat is at 627 °C.
(d) The atmosphere is at −23 °C, and the source of heat is at 727 °C.

K.6 (a) For each of the engines in Question K.5, find the temperature difference between the heat supply and the atmosphere in which the engine is working.
(b) On an ordinary piece of paper sketch two axes for a graph. Label the *x* axis **Temperature difference/K**. Mark on it, approximately, the positions for the temperature differences which you have just worked out. Label the *y* axis **Efficiency**. Mark on it the efficiencies which you worked out in Question K.5. You may include the origin, 0,0; because if the temperature difference is 0 K the engine will not work, and its efficiency will be 0. Sketch a graph of Efficiency against Temperature difference.
(c) What conclusion can you draw from the graph? In order to get the greatest efficiency what arrangement would you suggest for the temperature of the heat source and the temperature of the atmosphere in which the engine is working?
(d) In practice, there are limits to the temperature arrangements. Suggest some reasons why there are limits to the temperatures.

L Bimetal thermometers and fixed points

Bimetal thermometers were described on pages 30 to 31. You should read these pages.

Question L.1

A bimetal thermometer is placed in an ice/water mixture which has reached a constant temperature; and then it is placed in steam at 1 atmosphere pressure. The pointer moves through an angle of 50 degrees, in a clockwise direction.
(a) Use a protractor, and draw a semi-circular scale. Choose a suitable point on the semicircle, and mark it 0 **above** the semicircle. Now mark in **angle** degrees of 10, 20, 30, 40, 50, going clockwise. Also mark in 10 and 20 degrees going anticlockwise. Now **below** the semicircle mark in **temperature** degrees 0 °C and 100 °C at the appropriate points on the angle scale. Fill in the temperatures which correspond to the other angles.
(b) The thermometer is in a very hot store shed in midsummer, and the pointer is at an angle of 20 degrees. What is the temperature in the store?
(c) When the thermometer is placed in freshly poured concrete, the angle recorded is 11 degrees. What is the temperature of the concrete?

(d) The thermometer is in a store shed in midwinter and the pointer reads an angle of 4 degrees, left of the zero. What is the temperature?

L.2 A bimetal thermometer is designed for working over the range −20°C to +130°C. When it is placed in an ice/water mixture that has reached a constant temperature, and then in a steam chest at 1 atmosphere pressure, the pointer moves through an angle of 200 degrees clockwise.
  (a) What is the design range of the thermometer in kelvin?
  (b) Use a protractor and draw a full circle dial. Mark a scale in angle degrees every 10 degrees. Mark the Ice Point and the Steam Point in °C, and mark in the temperature scale from −20°C to +130°C.
  (c) The thermometer is used to measure the temperature of an oven in a site laboratory, and the pointer moves to an angle of 240 degrees. What is the temperature in the oven?
  (d) On a winter's day, the pointer is at an angle of 18 degrees **anticlockwise** from 0 on the angle scale. What is the temperature?

ANSWERS

A1 (a) 50 000 000 J (b) 23 000 000 J (c) 47 000 J
A2 (a) 45 000 kJ (b) 230 000 kJ (c) 470 kJ

B1 (a) 76.6 kW (b) 2.56 kW
B2 (a) 75 kW (b) 60 kW (c) 90 kW (d) 67.5 kW.

C1 (a) 22% (b) 31% (c) 20% (d) 33.3% (e) 23.0% (f) 34.0%
C2 (a) **1** 16.5 kW **2** 33.5 kW (b) 30.0%; 30.7%; 31.0%; 30.7%; 30.2%; 29.7%; 28.9%

D1 (a) 64.7 kJ (b) 44.6 kJ
D3 (a) Less (b) Greater
D4 (b) **1** 18.8% to 19.0% **2** 16.1% to 16.3%
D5 (a) **1** Yes **2** Yes (b) 35.2% (c) Exhaust, 39.1%; Engine output, 35.1%; Cooling water, 18.5%; Radiation and other, 5.1%; Lubricating oil, 2.2%

E1 (a) 12% (b) 14% (c) 27%
E2 (a) 40 kW (b) 20 kW

F1 (a) 1.7 mm (b) 1.2 mm (c) 0.6 mm
F2 (a) 4.8 mm (b) 2.4 mm (c) 0.2 mm
F3 (a) 6.0 mm (b) 3.6 mm
F4 (a) 7.2 mm (b) 12.00 mm
F5 (a) 30 K (b) 10.8 mm
F6 (a) 240 mm

G1 (a) 150 W (b) 150 J/s   **G2** 300 W
G3 45 W   **G4** (a) 150 W (b) 300 W
G5 (a) 50 W (b) 100 W

G6 (c) Worse (d) Slow down (e) Rise
G9 (g) **1** 100 W **2** 300 W

H1 A, 2.4 W; B, 1.2 W; C, 1.2 W; D, 1.2 W
H2 (a) **1** 500 W **2** 360 W (b) **1** 1 kW **2** 1.28 kW
H3 (a) **1** 21.2 W **2** 19.5 W (b) **1** 1100 W **2** 1600 W

I1 (a) **1** 100°C **2** 97°C **3** 90°C (b) **1** 107°C **2** 104.5°C **3** 98°C
I2 (a) 93.5°C (b) 89°C

J1 (a) 1440 kJ (b) 6720 kJ (c) 896 kJ (d) 8820 kJ
J2 (a) 780 kJ (b) 312 kJ
J3 (a) 21 kJ/s, 21 kW (b) 25.2 kJ/s, 25.2 kW (c) 3024 kJ/min, 50.4 kW (d) 1890 kJ/min, 31.5 kW
J4 (a) 585 W
J5 (a) **1** 0.192 m³/s **2** 11.5 m³/min (b) **1** 0.0308 m³/s **2** 1.85 m³/min

K1 (a) 273 K (b) 280 K (c) 290 K (d) 323 K (e) 373 K (f) 473 K (g) 533 K (h) 1273 K (i) 2973 K
K2 (a) 270 K (b) 263 K (c) 242 K (d) 123 K (e) 51 K (f) 0 K
K3 (a) 0°C (b) 10°C (c) 25°C (d) 100°C (e) 122°C (f) 327°C (g) 1100°C (h) 2227°C
K4 (a) −3°C (b) −13°C (c) −31°C (d) −123°C (e) −182°C (f) −263°C (g) −273°C
K5 (a) 25% (b) 50% (c) 67% (d) 75%
K6 (a) 100 K (b) 300 K (c) 600 K (d) 750 K

L1 (b) 40°C (c) 22°C (d) −8°C
L2 (a) 150 K (c) 120°C (d) −9°C

INDEX